AMADEUS

First produced at the National Theatre on 2nd November, 1979, with the following cast of characters:

The "**Venticelli**"	Dermot Crowley
	Donald Gee
Ignaz Greybig, valet to Salieri	Philip Locke
Antonio Salieri	Paul Scofield
Johann Kilian von Strack,	
Groom of the Imperial Chamber	Basil Henson
Count Orsini-Rosenberg,	
Director of the Imperial Opera	Andrew Cruickshank
Baron van Swieten,	
Prefect of the Imperial Library	Nicholas Selby
Constanze Weber	Felicity Kendal
Wolfgang Amadeus Mozart	Simon Callow
Major-Domo	William Sleigh
Joseph II, Emperor of Austria	John Normington
Servants and **Citizens of Vienna**	

Directed by Peter Hall

Design and lighting by John Bury

A revised version, upon which this Acting Edition is based, was subsequently presented at the National Theatre and transferred to Her Majesty's Theatre, London, on 2nd July, 1981, with the following cast of characters:

The "Venticelli"	Dermot Crowley
	Terry Wale
Salieri's Valet	David Stockton
Salieri's Cook	Ken Parry
Antonio Salieri	Frank Finlay
Joseph II, Emperor of Austria	John Harding
Johann Kilian von Strack,	
Groom of the Imperial Chamber	Brian Kent
Count Orsini-Rosenberg,	
Director of the Imperial Opera	Willoughby Goddard
Baron van Swieten,	
Prefect of the Imperial Library	Mark Dignam
Kapellmeister Bonno	Peter Gordon
Madame Salieri	Daphne Goddard
Katherina Cavalieri	Jane Morant
Constanze Weber	Morag Hood
Wolfgang Amadeus Mozart	Richard O'Callaghan
Major-Domo	Gary Hope
Servants and **Citizens of Vienna, a Priest**	

Directed by Peter Hall

Design and lighting by John Bury

The action takes place in Vienna

Time—November, 1823 and 1781–1791

AUTHOR'S NOTE

Amadeus can and should be played in a variety of settings. What is described in this text is to a large extent based on the exquisite formulation found for the play by the designer John Bury, helped into being by the director, Peter Hall. I was of course in enthusiastic agreement with this formulation, and set it down here as a tribute to exquisite work.

The set consisted basically of a handsome rectangle of patterned wood, its longest sides leading away from the viewer, set into a stage of ice-blue plastic. This surface shifted beguilingly under various lights played upon it, to show gunmetal grey, or azure, or emerald green, and reflected the actors standing upon it. The entire design was undeniably modern, yet it suggested without self-consciousness the age of the Rococo. Costumes and objects were sumptuously of the period, and should always be so wherever the play is produced.

The rectangle largely represented interiors: especially those of Salieri's apartments; Mozart's last apartment; assorted reception rooms, and opera houses. At the back stood a grand proscenium sporting gilded cherubs blowing huge trumpets, and supporting grand curtains of sky-blue, which could rise and part to reveal an enclosed space almost the width of the area downstage. Into this space superb backdrops were flown, and superb projections thrown, to show the scarlet boxes of theatres, or a vast wall of gold mirrors with an immense golden fireplace, representing the encrusted Palace of Schönbrunn. In it also appeared silhouettes of scandal-mongering citizens of Vienna, or the formal figures of the Emperor Joseph II of Austria and his brocaded courtiers. This wonderful upstage space, which was in effect an immense Rococo peep show, will be referred to throughout this text as the Light Box.

*   *   *   *

Changes of time and place are indicated throughout by changes of light. In reading the text it must be remembered that the action is wholly continuous. The asterisks which now and then divide the page indicate changes of scene, but there is to be no interruption. The scenes must flow into one another without pause from the beginning to the end of the play. Its fluidity is ensured by the use of Servants played by actors in eighteenth-century livery, whose role it is to move the furniture and carry on props with ease and correctness, while the action proceeds around them. Through a pleasant paradox of theatre their constant coming and going, bearing tables, chairs, or cloaks, should render them virtually invisible, and certainly unremarkable. This will aid the play to be acted throughout in its proper manner; with the sprung line, gracefulness and energy for which Mozart is so especially celebrated.

For
Robert
with love

ACT I

Vienna

On stage, before the House Lights are lowered, four objects are to be seen by the Audience. R of the wooden rectangle stands a table bearing a cake-stand. C, further upstage and also on the wood, stands a wheelchair of the eighteenth century, with its back to the Audience. L, on the reflecting plastic, stands a beautiful fortepiano in a marquetry case. Above the stage is suspended a large chandelier showing many globes of opaque glass. The curtains of the Light Box are open

The House Lights go down

In the darkness the Citizens of Vienna enter and take up their positions in the Light Box. Salieri also enters and sits in the wheelchair.

Savage whispers fill the theatre. We can distinguish nothing at first from this snake-like hissing save the word "SALIERI!" repeated here, there and everywhere around the theatre. Also the barely distinguishable word "ASSASSIN!"

The whispers overlap and increase in volume, slashing the air with wicked intensity. Then the Lights grow upstage to reveal the silhouettes of men and women dressed in top hats and skirts of the early nineteenth century—Citizens of Vienna, all crowded together in the Light Box, and uttering their scandal

Whisperers *Salieri! . . . Salieri! . . . Salieri!*

Downstage in the wheelchair with his back to the Audience, sits an old man. We can just see, as the Lights grow a little brighter, the top of his head encased in an old cap, and a shawl wrapped around his shoulders

Salieri! . . . Salieri! . . . Salieri!

Two middle-aged gentlemen hurry on from either side, also wearing the long cloaks and tall hats of the period. These are the two Venticelli: purveyors of fact, rumour and gossip throughout the play. They speak rapidly—in this first appearance extremely rapidly—so that the scene has the air of a fast and dreadful overture. Sometimes they speak to each other; sometimes to the Audience—but always with the urgency of men who have ever been first with the news

Venticello 1 I don't believe it.
Venticello 2 I don't believe it.

Venticello 1 I don't believe it.
Venticello 2 I don't believe it.
Whisperers *Salieri!*
Venticello 1 They say.
Venticello 2 I hear.
Venticello 1 I hear.
Venticello 2 They say.
Venticello 1 }
Venticello 2 } *(together)* { *I don't believe it!*
Whisperers *Salieri!*
Venticello 1 The whole city is talking.
Venticello 2 You hear it all over.
Venticello 1 The cafés.
Venticello 2 The Opera.
Venticello 1 The Prater.
Venticello 2 The gutter.
Venticello 1 They say even Metternich repeats it.
Venticello 2 They say even Beethoven, his old pupil.
Venticello 1 But why now?
Venticello 2 After so long?
Venticello 1 Thirty-two years!
Venticello 1 }
Venticello 2 } *(together)* { *I don't believe it!*
Whisperers SALIERI!
Venticello 1 They say he shouts it out all day!
Venticello 2 I hear he cries it out all night!
Venticello 1 Stays in his apartments.
Venticello 2 Never goes out.
Venticello 1 Not for a year now.
Venticello 2 Longer. Longer.
Venticello 1 Must be seventy.
Venticello 2 Older. Older.
Venticello 1 Antonio Salieri—
Venticello 2 The famous musician—
Venticello 1 Shouting it aloud!
Venticello 2 Crying it aloud!
Venticello 1 Impossible.
Venticello 2 Incredible.
Venticello 1 I don't believe it!
Venticello 2 I don't believe it!
Whisperers SALIERI!
Venticello 1 I know who *started* the tale!
Venticello 2 *I* know who started the tale!

*Two old men—one thin and dry, one very fat—walk on stage, from either
side: Salieri's Valet and Pastry Cook*

Venticello 1 *(indicating him)* The old man's Valet!
Venticello 2 *(indicating him)* The old man's Cook!

Venticello 1 The Valet hears him shouting!
Venticello 2 The Cook hears him crying!
Venticello 1 What a story!
Venticello 2 What a scandal!

The Venticelli move quickly upstage, one on either side, and each collects a silent informant. Venticello 1 walks down eagerly with the Valet; Venticello 2 walks down eagerly with the Cook

Venticello 1 (*to the Valet*) What does he say, your master?
Venticello 2 (*to the Cook*) What does he cry, the Kapellmeister?
Venticello 1 Alone in his house.
Venticello 2 All day and all night.
Venticello 1 What sins does he shout?
Venticello 2 The old fellow.
Venticello 1 The recluse.
Venticello 2 What horrors have you heard?
Venticello 1 ⎫ (*together*) ⎰ *Tell us! Tell us! Tell us at once! What does he cry?*
Venticello 2 ⎭   ⎱ *What does he cry? What does he cry?*

The Valet and the Cook gesture towards Salieri

Salieri (*in a great cry*) MOZART!!!

Silence

Venticello 1 (*whispering*) Mozart!
Venticello 2 (*whispering*) Mozart!
Salieri *Perdonami, Mozart! Il tuo assassino ti chiede perdono!*
Venticello 1 (*in disbelief*) Pardon, Mozart!
Venticello 2 (*in disbelief*) Pardon your assassin!
Venticello 1 ⎫ (*together*) ⎰ *God preserve us!*
Venticello 2 ⎭
Salieri *Pietà, Mozart. Mozart, pietà!*
Venticello 1 Mercy, Mozart!
Venticello 2 Mozart, have mercy!
Venticello 1 He speaks in Italian when excited!
Venticello 2 German when not!
Venticello 1 *Perdonami, Mozart!*
Venticello 2 Pardon your assassin!

The Valet and the Cook walk to either side of the stage, and stand still. Pause. The Venticelli cross themselves deeply shocked.

Venticello 1 There was talk once before, you know.
Venticello 2 Thirty-two years ago.
Venticello 1 When Mozart was dying.
Venticello 2 He claimed he'd been poisoned.
Venticello 1 Some said he accused a man.
Venticello 2 Some said that man was Salieri.
Venticello 1 But no-one believed it.
Venticello 2 They *knew* what he died of!

Venticello 1 Syphilis, surely.
Venticello 2 Like everybody else.

Pause

Venticello 1 (*slyly*) But what if Mozart was right?
Venticello 2 If he really *was* murdered?
Venticello 1 And by him. Our First Kapellmeister!
Venticello 2 Antonio Salieri!
Venticello 1 It can't possibly be true.
Venticello 2 It's not actually credible.
Venticello 1 Because *why*?
Venticello 2 Because why?
Venticello 1 ⎫ (*together*) ⎰ *Why on earth would he do it?*
Venticello 2 ⎭
Venticello 1 And why confess *now*?
Venticello 2 After thirty-two years!
Whisperers SALIERI!
Salieri *Mozart! Mozart! Perdonami!* ... *Il tuo assassino ti chiede perdono!*

Pause. They look at him—then at each other

Venticello 1 What do you think?
Venticello 2 What do you think?
Venticello 1 I don't believe it!
Venticello 2 *I* don't believe it!
Venticello 1 All the same ...
Venticello 2 Is it just possible?
Venticello 1 ⎫ (*whispering together*) ⎰ *Did he do it after all?*
Venticello 2 ⎭
Whisperers SALIERI!

The Venticelli exit

The Valet and the Cook remain on either side of the stage. Salieri swivels his wheelchair around and stares at us. We see a man of seventy in an old, stained dressing-robe, shawled. He rises and squints at the Audience as if trying to see it

*   *   *   *

Salieri's Apartments November 1823. The small hours

Salieri (*calling to the Audience*) *Vi saluto! Ombri del Futuro! Antonio Salieri—a vostro servizio!*

A clock outside in the street strikes three

I can almost see you in your ranks—waiting for your turn to live. Ghosts of the Future! Be visible. I beg you. Be visible. Come to this dusty old room—this time, the smallest hours of dark November, eighteen hundred and twenty-three—and be my confessors! Will you not enter this place and stay with me till dawn? Just till dawn—till six o'clock!

Whisperers *Salieri! ... Salieri! ...*

The curtains of the Light Box slowly descend on the Citizens of Vienna. Faint images of long windows are projected on to the silk

The Citizens of Vienna exit

Salieri Can you hear them? Vienna is a City of Slander. Everyone tells tales here: even my servants. I keep only two now—(*he indicates them*)—they've been with me ever since I came here, fifty years ago. The Keeper of the Razor: the Maker of the Cakes. One keeps me tidy, the other keeps me full. (*To them*) Leave me, both of you! Tonight I do not go to bed at all!

They react in surprise

Return here tomorrow morning at six precisely—to shave, to feed, your capricious master! (*He smiles at them both and claps his hands in gentle dismissal*) Via. Via, via, via! Grazie!

They bow, bewildered, and leave the stage

How surprised they are! ... They'll be even more surprised tomorrow: indeed they will! (*He peers hard at the Audience, trying to see it*) Oh, won't you appear? I need you—desperately! Those about to die implore you! What must I do to make you visible? Raise you up in the flesh to be my last, last audience? ... Does it take an Invocation? That's how it's always done in opera! Ah yes, of course: that's it. An *Invocation*. The only way. (*He rises*) Let me try to conjure you *now*—Ghosts of the distant Future—so I can see you.

He gets out of the wheelchair and huddles over to the fortepiano. He stands at the instrument and begins to sing in a high cracked voice, interrupting himself at the end of each sentence with figurations on the keyboard in the manner of a recitativo secco. During this the House Lights slowly come up to illuminate the Audience

(*Singing*)   Ghosts of the Future!
                   Shades of Time to come!
                   So much more unavoidable than those of time gone by!
                   Appear with what sympathy incarnation may endow
                       you!
                   Appear you—
                   The yet-to-be-born!
                   The yet-to-hate!
                   The yet-to-*kill*!
                   Appear—posterity!

The House Lights reach maximum. They stay like this during all of the following

(*Speaking again*) There. It worked. I can see you! That is the result of proper training. I was taught Invocation by Chevalier Gluck, who was a true master at it. He had to be. In his day that is what people went to the opera for: the raising of gods, and ghosts ... Nowadays, since Rossini became the rage, they prefer to watch the antics of hairdressers.

Pause

Scusate. Invocation is an exhausting business I need refreshment. (*He goes to the cake-stand*) It's a little repellent, I admit—but actually the first sin I have to confess to you is Gluttony. Sticky gluttony at that. Infantine—Italian gluttony! The truth is that all my life I have never been able to conquer a lust for the sweetmeats of Northern Italy where I was born. From the ages of three to seventy-three my entire career has been conducted to the taste of almonds sprinkled with sifted sugar. (*Lustfully*) Milanese biscuits! Siena macaroons! Snow dumplings with pistachio sauce! ... Do not judge me too harshly for this. All men harbour patriotic feelings of some kind ... My parents were Italian subjects of the Austrian Empire, a Lombardy merchant and his Lombardy wife. Their notion of place was the tiny town of Legnago—which I could not wait to leave. Their notion of God was a superior Hapsburg emperor inhabiting a Heaven only slightly further off than Vienna. All they asked of Him was to keep them forever unnoticed—preserved in mediocrity. My own requirements were very different.

Pause

I wanted fame. Not to deceive you. I wanted to *blaze*, like a comet, across the firmament of Europe. Yet only in one especial way. Music. Absolute music! A note of music is either right or wrong—*absolutely*! Not even time can alter that: music is God's art. (*Excited by the recollection*) Already when I was ten a spray of sounded notes would make me dizzy almost to falling! By twelve I was stumbling about the countryside, humming my arias and anthems to the Lord! My one desire was to join all the composers who had celebrated God's glory through the long Italian past! ... Every Sunday I saw Him in church, painted on the flaking wall. I don't mean Christ. The Christs of Lombardy are simpering sillies with lambkins on their sleeves. No: I mean an old candle-smoked God in a mulberry robe, staring at the world with dealer's eyes. Tradesmen had put him up there. Those eyes made bargains, real and irreversible. "You give me so— I'll give you so! No more. No less!" (*He eats a sweet biscuit in his excitement*) One night I went to see Him—and made a bargain with Him myself! I was a sober sixteen, filled with a desperate sense of right. I knelt before the God of Bargains, and I prayed with all my soul.

He kneels. The House Lights go out slowly

"*Signore*, let me be a composer! Grant me sufficient fame to enjoy it. In return I will live with virtue. I will be chaste. I will strive to better the lot of my fellows. And I will honour You with much music all the days of my life!" As I said "Amen", I saw His eyes flare. (*As "God"*) "*Bene.* Go forth Antonio. Serve Me and mankind—and you will be blessed!" ... "*Grazie!*" I called back. "I am Your servant for life!" (*He gets to his feet again*) The very next day, a family friend suddenly appeared—out of the blue—took me off to Vienna and paid for me to study music!

Pause

Shortly afterwards I met the Emperor of Austria, who favoured me. *Clearly my bargain had been accepted!*

Pause

The same year I left Italy, a young prodigy was touring Europe. A miraculous virtuoso aged ten years. Wolfgang Amadeus Mozart.

Pause. He smiles at the Audience. Pause

And now! Gracious ladies! Obliging gentlemen! I present to you—for one performance only—my last composition, entitled *The Death of Mozart— or Did I Do It?* . . . Dedicated to posterity on this—the last night of my life!

He bows deeply, undoing as he does so the buttons of his old dressing-robe. When he straightens himself—divesting himself of this drab outer garment and his cap—he is a young man in the prime of life, wearing a sky-blue coat and the elegant decent clothes of a successful composer of the seventeen-eighties

*   *   *   *

Transformation to the Eighteenth Century

Music sounds softly in the background: a serene piece for strings by Salieri

Servants enter. One takes away the dressing-robe, cap and shawl; another places on the table a wig-stand bearing a powdered wig; a third brings on an upright chair and places it UR. *They take the wheelchair and exit*

The curtains of the Light Box rise and part to show the Emperor Joseph II and his Court bathed in golden light, against a golden background of mirrors and an immense golden fireplace. His Majesty is seated, holding a rolled paper, listening to the music. Also listening are Count von Strack; Count Orsini-Rosenberg; Baron van Swieten; and an anonymous Priest dressed in a soutane

An old wigged courtier, Kapellmeister Bonno, enters and takes his place at the keyboard

Salieri takes his wig from the stand

Salieri (*in a young man's voice: vigorous and confident*) The place throughout is Vienna. The year—to begin with—seventeen eighty-one. The age still that of the Enlightenment: that clear time before the guillotine fell in France and cut all our lives in half. I am thirty-one. Already a prolific composer to the Hapsburg court. I own a respectable house and a respectable wife—Teresa.

Teresa enters R; *a padded, placid lady who seats herself uprightly in the upstage chair*

I do not mock her, I assure you. I required only one quality in a domestic companion:—lack of fire. And in that omission Teresa was conspicuous. (*Ceremoniously he puts on his powdered wig*) I also had a prize pupil: Katherina Cavalieri.

Katherina, a beautiful girl of twenty, swirls on L and stands by the fortepiano

At the same time the music becomes vocal: faintly we hear a soprano singing a concert aria. Like Teresa's, Katherina's part is mute—but she energetically mimes her rapturous singing. At the keyboard old Bonno accompanies her appreciatively

She was a bubbling student with merry eyes and a sweet, eatable mouth. I was very much in love with Katherina—or at least in lust. But because of my vow to God, I had never laid a finger upon the girl—except occasionally to depress her diaphragm in the way of teaching her to sing. My ambition burned with an unquenchable flame. Its chief goal was the post of First Royal Kapellmeister, then held by Giuseppe Bonno—*(indicating him)*—seventy years old, and apparently immortal.

All on stage, save Salieri, suddenly freeze. He speaks very directly to the Audience

You, when you come, will be told that we musicians of the eighteenth century were no better than servants: the willing slaves of the well-to-do. This is quite true. It is also quite false. Yes, we were servants. But we were learned servants! And we used our learning to celebrate men's average lives!

A grander music sounds

The Emperor remains seated, but the other four men in the Light Box—von Strack, Orsini-Rosenberg, van Swieten and the Priest—come slowly out on to the main stage and process imposingly down it, and around it, and up it again to return to their places

The Priest goes off, as do Teresa on her side and Katherina on hers. Bonno also exits

(Over this) We took unremarkable men: usual bankers, run-of-the-mill priests, ordinary soliders and statesmen and wives—and sacramentalized their mediocrity. We smoothed their noons with strings *divisi!*, we pierced their nights with *chittarini*! We gave them processions for their strutting—serenades for their rutting—high horns for their hunting, and drums for their wars! Trumpets sounded when they entered the world, and trombones groaned when they left it! The savour of their days remains behind because of *us*, our music still remembered while their politics are long forgotten.

The Emperor hands his rolled paper to von Strack and goes off

In the Light Box are left standing, like three icons, Orsini-Rosenberg, plump and supercilious, aged sixty; von Strack, stiff and proper, aged fifty-five; van Swieten, cultivated and serious, aged fifty. The Lights go down on them a little

Tell me, before you call us servants, who served whom? And who I wonder, in your generations, will immortalize *you*?

The two Venticelli come on quickly downstage, from either side. They are now be-wigged also, and are dressed well, in the style of the late eighteenth century. Their manner is more confidential than before

Venticello 1 (*to Salieri*) Sir!
Venticello 2 (*to Salieri*) Sir!
Venticello 1 Sir. Sir.
Venticello 2 Sir. Sir. Sir.

Salieri bids them wait for a second

Salieri I was the most successful young musician in the city of musicians. And now suddenly, without warning——

They approach him eagerly, from either side

Venticello 1 Mozart!
Venticello 2 Mozart!
Venticello 1 ⎱
                       (*together*)⎱ *Mozart has come!*
Venticello 2 ⎰
Salieri These are my *Venticelli*. My "Little Winds" as I call them. (*He gives each a coin from his pocket*) The secret of successful living in a large city is always to know to the minute what is being done behind your back.
Venticello 1 He's left Salzburg.
Venticello 2 Means to give concerts.
Venticello 1 Asking for subscribers.
Salieri I'd known of him for years, of course. Tales of his prowess were told all over Europe.
Venticello 1 They say he wrote his first symphony at five.
Venticello 2 I hear his first concerto at four.
Venticello 1 A full opera at fourteen.
Venticello 2 *Mitridate, King of Pontus.*
Salieri (*to them*) How old is he now?
Venticello 2 Twenty-five.
Salieri (*carefully*) And how long is he remaining?
Venticello 1 He's not departing.
Venticello 2 He's here to stay.

The Venticelli glide off

Black-out

*   *   *   *

The Palace of Schönbrunn

The Lights come up on the three stiff figures of Orsini-Rosenberg, the Director of the Opera, von Strack, the Royal Chamberlain, and van Swieten, Prefect of the Imperial Library, standing upstage in the Light Box. Von Strack hands the paper he has received from the Emperor to Orsini-Rosenberg. Salieri remains downstage

Von Strack (*to Orsini-Rosenberg*) You are required to commission a comic opera in German from Herr Mozart.

Salieri (*to the Audience*) Johann von Strack. Royal Chamberlain. A court official to his collar bone.

Orsini-Rosenberg (*loftily*) Why in German? Italian is the only possible language for opera!

Salieri Count Orsini-Rosenberg. Director of the Opera. Benevolent to all things Italian—especially myself.

Von Strack (*stiffly*) The idea of a national opera is dear to His Majesty's heart. He desires to hear pieces in good plain German.

Van Swieten Yes, but why comic? It is not the function of music to be funny.

Salieri Baron van Swieten. Prefect of the Imperial Library. Ardent Freemason. Yet to find anything funny. Known for his enthusiasm for old-fashioned music as "Lord Fugue".

Van Swieten I heard last week a remarkable *serious* opera from Mozart: *Idomeneo, King of Crete.*

Orsini-Rosenberg I heard that too. A young fellow trying to impress beyond his abilities. Too much spice. Too many notes.

Von Strack (*firmly, to Orsini-Rosenberg*) Nevertheless, kindly convey the commission to him today.

Orsini-Rosenberg (*taking the paper reluctantly*) I believe we are going to have trouble with this young man. (*Orsini-Rosenberg leaves the Light Box and strolls down the stage to Salieri*) He was a child prodigy. That always spells trouble. His father is Leopold Mozart, a pedantic Salzburg musician in the service of the Archbishop. He dragged the boy endlessly round Europe making him play the keyboard blindfold, with one finger, and that sort of thing. (*To Salieri*) All prodigies are hateful—*non è vero, Compositore?*

Salieri *Divengono sempre sterili con gli anni.*

Orsini-Rosenberg *Precisamente. Precisamente.*

Von Strack (*calling suspiciously*) What are you saying?

Orsini-Rosenberg (*airily*) Nothing, Herr Chamberlain! ... *Niente, Signor Pomposo!* ...

Orsini-Rosenberg strolls on out. Von Strack strides off irritated

Van Swieten (*coming downstage*) We meet tomorrow, I believe, on your committee to devise pensions for old musicians.

Salieri (*deferentially*) It's most gracious of you to attend, Baron.

Van Swieten You're a worthy man, Salieri. You should join our Brotherhood of Masons. We would welcome you warmly.

Salieri I would be honoured, Baron!

Van Swieten If you wished I could arrange initiation into my lodge.

Salieri That would be more than my due.

Van Swieten Nonsense. We embrace men of talent of all conditions. I may invite young Mozart also: dependent on the impression he makes.

Salieri (*bowing*) Of course, Baron.

Van Swieten goes out

(*To the Audience*) Honour indeed. In those days almost every man of influence in Vienna was a Mason—and the Baron's lodge by far the most fashionable. As for young Mozart, I confess I was alarmed by his coming. He was praised altogether too much.

The Venticelli hurry in from either side

Venticello 1 Such gaiety of spirit!

Venticello 2 Such ease of manner!

Venticello 1 Such natural charm!

Salieri (*to the Venticelli*) Really? Where does he live?

Venticello 1 Peter Platz.

Venticello 2 Number eleven.

Venticello 1 The landlady is Madame Weber.

Venticello 2 A real bitch.

Venticello 1 Takes in male lodgers, and has a tribe of daughters.

Venticello 2 Mozart was engaged to one of them before.

Venticello 1 A soprano called Aloysia.

Venticello 2 She jilted him.

Venticello 1 Now he's after another sister.

Venticello 2 Constanze!

Salieri You mean he was actually engaged to one sister and now wants to marry another?

Venticello 1
Venticello 2 } (*together*) {Exactly!

Venticello 1 Her mother's pushing marriage.

Venticello 2 His *father* isn't!

Venticello 1 Daddy is worried sick!

Venticello 2 Writes him every day from Salzburg!

Salieri (*to them*) I want to meet him.

Venticello 1 He'll be at the Baroness Waldstädten's tomorrow night.

Salieri *Grazie.*

Venticello 2 Some of his music is to be played.

Salieri (*to both*) *Restiamo in contatto.*

Venticello 1
Venticello 2 } (*together*) {*Certamente, Signore!*

They go off

Salieri (*to the Audience*) So to the Baroness Waldstädten's I went. That night changed my life.

                    *   *   *   *

The Library of the Baroness Waldstädten

In the Light Box, the background shows two elegantly curtained windows surrounded by handsome subdued wallpaper

Two Servants bring on a large table loaded with cakes and desserts and place it c. *Two more carry on a grand, high-backed wing-chair which they place ceremoniously* DR *near the small table. They take the wig-stand from the table and exit*

Salieri (*to the Audience*) I entered the library to take first a little refreshment. My generous hostess always put out the most delicious confections in that room whenever she knew I was coming. *Sorbetti—caramelli*—and most especially a miraculous *crema al mascarpone*—which is simply cream cheese mixed with granulated sugar and suffused with rum—that was totally irresistible! (*He takes a little bowl of it from the cake-stand and sits in the wing-chair, facing out front. Thus seated, he is invisible to anyone entering from upstage*) I had just sat down in a high-backed chair to consume this paradisal dish—unobservable as it happened to anyone who might come in.

Off-stage, noises are heard

Constanze (*off*) Squeak! Squeak! Squeak!

Constanze runs on from upstage: a pretty girl in her early twenties, full of high spirits. At this second she is pretending to be a mouse. She runs across the stage in her gay party dress, and hides under the fortepiano

Suddenly a small, pallid, large-eyed man in a showy wig and a showy set of clothes runs in after her and freezes C, *as a cat would freeze, hunting a mouse. This is Wolfgang Amadeus Mozart. As we get to know him through his next scenes, we discover several things about him: he is an extremely restless man, his hands and feet in almost continuous motion; his voice is light and high; and he is possessed of an unforgettable giggle—piercing and infantile*

Mozart Miaouw!
Constanze (*betraying where she is*) Squeak!
Mozart Miaouw! Miaouw! Miaouw!

The composer drops on all fours and, wrinkling his face, begins spitting and stalking his prey. The mouse—giggling with excitement—breaks her cover and dashes across the floor. The cat pursues. Almost at the chair where Salieri sits concealed, the mouse turns at bay. The cat stalks her—nearer and nearer—in its knee-breeches and elaborate coat

Mozart I'm going to pounce-bounce! I'm going to scrunch-munch! I'm going to chewpoo my little mouse-wouse! I'm going to tear her to bits with my paws-claws!
Constanze No!
Mozart Paws-claws, paws-claws, paws-claws! OHH! . . .

He falls on her. She screams

Salieri (*to the Audience*) Before I could rise, it had become difficult to do so. (*He surreptitiously places the bowl on the small table*)
Mozart I'm going to bite you in half with my fangs-wangs! My little Stanzerl-wanzerl-banzerl!

She giggles delightedly, lying prone beneath him

You're trembling! . . . I think you're frightened of puss-wuss! . . . I think you're scared to death! (*Intimately*) I think you're going to shit yourself.

She squeals, but is not really shocked

In a moment it's going to be on the floor!
Constanze Ssh! Someone'll hear you!

He imitates the noise of a fart

Stop it, Wolferl! Ssh!

Mozart Here it comes now! I can hear it *coming*! . . . Oh what a melancholy note! Something's dropping from your boat!

Another fart noise, slower. Constanze shrieks with amusement

Constanze Stop it now! It's stupid! Really *stupid*!

Salieri sits appalled

Mozart Hey—hey—what's Trazom!
Constanze What?
Mozart T-R-A-Z-O-M. What's that mean?
Constanze How should *I* know?
Mozart It's Mozart spelt backwards—shit-wit! If you ever married me, you'd be Constanze Trazom.
Constanze No, I wouldn't.
Mozart Yes, you would. Because I'd want everything backwards once I was married. I'd want to lick my wife's arse instead of her face.
Constanze You're not going to lick anything at this rate. Your father's never going to give his consent to us.

The sense of fun deserts him instantly

Mozart And who cares about his consent?
Constanze *You* do. You care very much. You wouldn't do it without it.
Mozart Wouldn't I?
Constanze No, you wouldn't. Because you're too scared of him. I know what he says about me. (*In a solemn voice*) "If you marry that dreadful girl, you'll end up lying on straw with beggars for children."
Mozart (*impulsively*) Marry me!
Constanze Don't be silly.
Mozart Marry me!
Constanze Are you serious?
Mozart (*defiantly*) Yes! . . . Answer me this minute: yes or no! Say yes, then I can go home, climb into bed—shit over the mattress and shout "I *did* it!" (*He rolls on top of her delightedly, uttering his high, whinnying giggle*)

The Major-Domo of the house stalks in upstage

Major-Domo (*imperviously*) Her ladyship is ready to commence.
Mozart Ah! . . . Yes! . . . Good!

He picks himself up, embarrassed, and helps Constanze to rise

(*With an attempt at dignity*) Come, my dear. The music waits!
Constanze (*suppressing giggles*) Oh, by all means—Herr Trazom!

He takes her arm. They prance off together, followed by the disapproving Major-Domo

Salieri (*shaken; to the Audience*) And then, right away, the concert began. I heard it through the door—some serenade: at first only vaguely—too horrified to attend. But presently the sound insisted—a solemn Adagio, in E Flat.

The Adagio of the Serenade for Thirteen Wind Instruments (K. 361) begins to sound. Quietly and quite slowly, seated in the wing-chair, Salieri speaks over the music

It started simply enough: just a pulse in the lowest registers—bassoons and basset horns—like a rusty squeezebox. It would have been comic except for the slowness, which gave it instead a sort of serenity. And then suddenly, high above it, sounded a single note on the oboe.

We hear it

It hung there unwavering—piercing me through—till breath could hold it no longer, and a clarinet withdrew it out of me, and sweetened it into a phrase of such delight it had me trembling. The light flickered in the room. My eyes clouded! (*With ever-increasing emotion and vigour*) The squeezebox groaned louder, and over it the higher instruments wailed and warbled, throwing lines of sound around me—long lines of pain around and through me—Ah, the pain! Pain as I had never known it. I called up to my sharp old God "*What is this? ... What?*" But the squeezebox went on and on, and the pain cut deeper into my shaking head until suddenly I was running——

He bolts out of the chair and runs across the stage in a fever, to C. *Behind him in the Light Box the Library fades into a street scene at night: small houses under a rent sky. The music continues fainter, underneath*

—dashing through the side-door, stumbling downstairs into the street, into the cold night, gasping for life. (*Calling up in agony*) "*What?! What is this? Tell me, Signore!* What is this *pain*? What is this *need* in the sound? Forever unfulfillable yet fulfilling him who hears it, utterly. Is it *Your* need! *Can it be Yours?*" ...

Pause

Dimly the music sounded from the salon above. Dimly the stars shone on the empty street. I was suddenly frightened. It seemed to me I had heard a voice of God—and that it issued from a creature whose own voice I had also heard—and it was the voice of an obscene child!

The Lights change. The street scene fades

*   *   *   *

Salieri's Apartments

It remains dark

Salieri I ran home and buried my fear in work. More pupils—till there were thirty and forty. More committees toiling long hours to help musicians! More motets and anthems to God's glory. And at night I prayed for just one thing. (*He kneels desperately*) "Let your voice enter *me*! Let *me* be your conduct! ... Let *me*!" (*Pause. He rises*) As for Mozart, I avoided meeting him—and sent out my "Little Winds" for whatever scores of his could be found.

The Venticelli come in with manuscripts. Salieri sits at the fortepiano, and they show him the music alternately, as Servants unobtrusively remove the large table and wing-chair

Venticello 1 Six fortepiano Sonatas composed in Munich.
Salieri Clever.
Venticello 2 Two in Mannheim.
Salieri They were all clever.
Venticello 1 A Parisian Symphony.
Salieri (*to the Audience*) And yet they seemed to me completely empty!
Venticello 1 A Divertimento in D.
Salieri The same.
Venticello 2 A Cassazione in G.
Salieri Conventional.
Venticello 1 A Grand Litany in E Flat.
Salieri Even boring. (*To the Audience*) The productions of a precocious youngster—Leopold Mozart's swanky son—nothing more. That Serenade was obviously an exception in his work: the sort of accident which might visit any composer on a lucky day!

The Venticelli go off with the music

Had I in fact been simply taken by surprise that the filthy creature could write music at all? ... Suddenly I felt immensely cheered! I would seek him out and welcome him myself to Vienna!

*   *   *   *

The Palace of Schönbrunn

The Lights change quickly. In the Light Box the Emperor is revealed standing in bright light before the gilded mirrors and the fireplace, attended by Chamberlain von Strack. His Majesty is a dapper, cheerful figure, aged forty, largely pleased with himself and the world

Downstage, from opposite sides, van Swieten and Orsini-Rosenberg hurry on

Joseph Fêtes and fireworks, gentlemen! Mozart is here! He's waiting below!
All (*bowing*) Majesty!
Joseph *Je suis follement impatient!*

Salieri (*to the Audience*) The Emperor Joseph the Second of Austria. Son of Maria Theresa. Brother of Marie Antoinette. Adorer of music—provided that it made no demands upon the royal brain. (*To the Emperor; deferentially*) Majesty, I have written a little march in Mozart's honour. May I play it as he comes in?

Joseph By all means, Court Composer. What a delightful idea! Have you met him yet?

Salieri Not yet, Majesty.

Joseph Fêtes and fireworks, what fun! Strack, bring him up at once.

Von Strack goes off

The Emperor comes on to the stage proper

Mon Dieu, I wish we could have a competition! Mozart against some other virtuoso. Two keyboards in contest. Wouldn't that be fun, Baron?

Van Swieten (*stiffly*) Not to me, Majesty. In my view, musicians are not horses to be run against one another.

Slight pause

Joseph Ah. Well—there it is.

Von Strack returns

Von Strack Herr Mozart, Majesty.

Joseph Ah! Splendid! . . .

Conspiratorially he signs to Salieri, who moves quickly to the fortepiano

Court-Composer—allons! (*To von Strack*) Admit him, please.

Instantly Salieri sits at the instrument and strikes up his march on the keyboard

At the same moment Mozart struts in, wearing an extremely ornate surcoat, with dress-sword

The Emperor stands DC, his back to the Audience, and as Mozart approaches he signs to him to halt and listen. Bewildered, Mozart does so—becoming aware of Salieri playing his "March of Welcome". It is an extremely banal piece, vaguely—but only vaguely—reminiscent of another march to become very famous later on. All stand frozen in attitudes of listening, until Salieri comes to a finish. Applause

(*To Salieri*) Charming . . . Comme d'habitude! (*He turns and extends his hand to be kissed*) Mozart.

Mozart approaches and kneels extravagantly

Mozart Majesty! Your Majesty's humble slave! Let me kiss your royal hand a hundred thousand times!

He kisses it greedily, over and over, until its owner withdraws it in embarrassment

Joseph *Non, non, s'il vous plaît!* A little less enthusiasm, I beg you. Come sir. *Levez-vous!*

He assists Mozart to rise

You will not recall it, but the last time we met you were also on the floor! My sister remembers it to this day. This young man—all of six years old, mind you—slipped on the floor at Schönbrunn—came a nasty purler on his little head ... Have I told you this before?

Orsini-Rosenberg *(hastily)* No, Majesty!
Von Strack *(hastily)* No, Majesty!
Salieri *(hastily)* No, Majesty!
Joseph Well, my sister Antoinette runs forward and picks him up herself. And do you know what he does? Jumps right into her arms—hoopla, just like that!—kisses her on both cheeks and says "Will you marry me: yes or no?"

The courtiers laugh politely. Mozart emits his high-pitched giggle. The Emperor is clearly startled by it

I do not mean to embarrass you, Herr Mozart. You know everyone here, surely?

Mozart Yes, Sire. *(Bowing elaborately to Orsini-Rosenberg)* Herr Director! *(To van Swieten)* Herr Prefect.
Joseph But not, I think, our esteemed Court Composer! ... A most serious omission! No-one who cares for art can afford not to know Herr Salieri. He wrote that exquisite little "March of Welcome" for you.
Salieri It was a trifle, Majesty.
Joseph Nevertheless ...
Mozart *(to Salieri)* I'm overwhelmed, *Signore!*
Joseph Ideas simply pour out of him—don't they, Strack?
Von Strack Endlessly, Sire. *(As if tipping him)* Well done, Salieri.
Joseph Let it be my pleasure then to introduce you! Court Composer Salieri—Herr Mozart of Salzburg!
Salieri *(sleekly; to Mozart)* *Finalmente. Che gioia. Che diletto straordinario.*

Salieri gives him a prim bow and presents the copy of his music to the other composer, who accepts it with a flood of Italian

Mozart *Grazie, Signore! Mille millione di venvenuti! Sono commosso! È un onore eccezionale incontrala! Compositore brillante e famossissimo! (He makes an elaborate and showy bow in return)*
Salieri *(drily)* *Grazie.*
Joseph Tell me, Mozart, have you received our commission for the opera?
Mozart Indeed I have, Majesty! I am so grateful I can hardly speak! ... I swear to you that you will have the best—the most perfect entertainment ever offered a monarch. I've already found a libretto.
Orsini-Rosenberg *(startled)* Have you? I didn't hear of this!
Mozart Forgive me, Herr Director, I entirely omitted to tell you.
Orsini-Rosenberg May I ask why?
Mozart It didn't seem very important.

Orsini-Rosenberg Not important?

Mozart Not really, no.

Orsini-Rosenberg (*irritated*) It is important to *me*, Herr Mozart.

Mozart (*embarrassed*) Yes, I see that. Of course.

Orsini-Rosenberg And who, pray, is it by?

Mozart Stephanie.

Orsini-Rosenberg A most unpleasant man.

Mozart But a brilliant writer.

Orsini-Rosenberg Do you think?

Mozart The story is really amusing, Majesty. The whole plot is set in a—(*he giggles*)—in a ... It's set in a ...

Joseph (*eagerly*) Where? Where is it set?

Mozart It's—it's—rather saucy, Majesty!

Joseph Yes, yes! Where?

Mozart Well it's actually set in a *seraglio*.

Joseph A what?

Mozart A pasha's harem. (*He giggles wildly*)

Orsini-Rosenberg And you imagine that is a suitable subject for performance at a national theatre?

Mozart (*in a panic*) Yes! No! Yes, I mean yes, yes I do. Why not? It's very funny, it's amusing ... On my honour, Majesty, there's nothing offensive in it. Nothing offensive in the world. It's full of proper German virtues, I swear it! ...

Salieri (*blandly*) Scusate, Signore, but what are those? Being a foreigner I'm not sure.

Joseph You are being *cattivo*, Court Composer.

Salieri Not at all, Majesty.

Joseph Come then, Mozart. Name us a proper German virtue!

Mozart Love, Sire. I have yet to see that expressed in any opera.

Van Swieten Well answered, Mozart.

Salieri (*smiling*) Scusate. I was under the impression one rarely saw anything *else* expressed in opera.

Mozart I mean manly love, *Signore*. Not male soparanos screeching. Or stupid couples rolling their eyes. All that absurd Italian rubbish.

Pause. Tension

I mean the real thing.

Joseph And do you know the real thing yourself, Herr Mozart?

Mozart Under your pardon, I think I do, Majesty. (*He gives a short giggle*)

Joseph Bravo. When do you think it will be done?

Mozart The first act is already finished.

Joseph But it can't be more than two weeks since you started!

Mozart Composing is not hard when you have the right audience to please, Sire.

Van Swieten A charming reply, Majesty.

Joseph Indeed, Baron. Fêtes and fireworks! I see we are going to have fêtes and fireworks! *Au revoir, Monsieur Mozart. Soyez bienvenu à la court.*

Mozart (*with expert rapidity*) Majesté!—je suis comblé d'honneur d'être

*accepté dans la maison du Père de tous les musiciens! Servir un monarque
aussi plein de discernement que votre Majesté, c'est un honneur qui dépasse
le sommet de mes dus!*

A pause. The Emperor is taken aback by this flood of French

Joseph Ah. Well—there it is. I'll leave you gentlemen to get better
acquainted.
Salieri Good-day, Majesty.
Mozart *Votre Majesté.*

Salieri and Mozart bow

Joseph goes out

Orsini-Rosenberg Good-day to you.
Von Strack Good-day.

Orsini-Rosenberg and von Strack follow the Emperor out

Van Swieten (*warmly shaking his hand*) Welcome, Mozart. I shall see much
more of you. Depend on it!
Mozart Thank you. (*He bows*)

Van Swieten goes out

Salieri *Bene.*
Mozart *Bene.*
Salieri I too wish you success with your opera.
Mozart I'll have it. It's going to be superb. I must tell you I have already
found the most excellent singer for the leading part.
Salieri Oh: who is that?
Mozart Her name is Cavalieri. Katherina Cavalieri. She's really German,
but she thinks it will advance her career if she sports an Italian name.
Salieri She's quite right. It was my idea. She is in fact my prize pupil.
Actually she's a very innocent child. Silly in the way of young singers—
but, you know, she's only twenty.

*Without emphasis Mozart freezes his movements and Salieri takes one easy
step forward to make a fluent aside*

(*To the Audience*) I had kept my hands off Katherina. Yes! But, I could
not bear to think of anyone else's upon her—least of all his!
Mozart (*unfreezing*) You're a good fellow, Salieri! And that's a jolly little
thing you wrote for me.
Salieri It was my pleasure.
Mozart Let's see if I can remember it. May I?
Salieri By all means. It's yours.
Mozart *Grazie, Signore.*

*Mozart tosses the manuscript on to the lid of the fortepiano where he cannot
see it, sits at the instrument, and plays Salieri's "March of Welcome"
perfectly from memory—at first slowly, recalling it—but on the reprise of the
tune, very much faster*

The rest is just the same, isn't it? (*He finishes it with insolent speed*)

Salieri You have a remarkable memory.

Mozart (*delighted with himself*) Grazie ancora, Signore! (*He plays the opening seven bars again, but this time stops on the interval of the fourth, and sounds it again with displeasure*) It doesn't really *work*, that fourth—does it? ... Let's try the third above ... (*He does so—and smiles happily*) Ah yes! ... Good! ...

He repeats the new interval, leading up to it smartly with the well-known military-trumpet arpeggio which characterizes the celebrated march from The Marriage of Figaro, "Non piu andrai". Then, using the interval—tentatively—delicately—one note at a time, in the treble—he steals into the famous tune itself. On and on he plays, improvizing happily what is virtually the march we know now, laughing gleefully each time he comes to the amended interval of a third. Salieri watches him with an answering smile painted on his face. Mozart's playing grows more and more exhibitionistic—revealing to the Audience the formidable virtuoso he is. The whole time he himself remains totally oblivious to the offence he is giving. Finally he finishes the march with a series of triumphant flourishes and chords!

An ominous pause

Salieri *Scusate.* I must go.

Mozart Really? (*Springing up and indicating the keyboard*) Why don't *you* try a variation?

Salieri Thank you, but I must attend on the Emperor.

Mozart Ah.

Salieri It has been delightful to meet you.

Mozart For me too! ... And thanks for the march!

Mozart picks up the manuscript from the top of the fortepiano and marches happily offstage

A slight pause. Salieri moves toward the Audience. The Lights go down around him

Salieri (*to the Audience*) Was it then—so early—that I began to have thoughts of murder? ... Of course not: at least not in life. In art it was a different matter. I decided I would compose a huge tragic opera: something to astonish the world!—and I knew my theme. I would set the legend of Danaius, who, for a monstrous crime was chained to a rock for eternity—his head repeatedly struck by lightning! Wickedly I saw Mozart in that position. In reality the man was in no danger at all ... Not yet.

*   *   *   *

The First Performance of The Abduction From The Seraglio

The Lights change, and the stage instantly turns into an eighteenth-century theatre. The Light Box background shows a line of softly gleaming chandeliers

The Servants bring on chairs and benches and place them c *facing the*

Audience, making a front row of seven chairs with another placed a little behind this and the benches at the back. When this is completed they exit

The Emperor, von Strack, Orsini-Rosenberg and van Swieten enter and sit in that order. Kapellmeister Bonno and Teresa Salieri come on and sit next to them, followed by Constanze who sits a little behind them. The Citizens of Vienna enter and sit on the benches

Salieri The first performance of *The Abduction From The Seraglio*. The German expression of manly love.

Mozart comes on briskly, wearing a gaudy new coat and a new powdered wig. He struts quickly to the fortepiano, sits at it and mimes conducting. Salieri sits nearby, next to his wife, and watches Mozart intently. Everyone else stares out front at the Audience as if watching the opera

He himself contrived to wear for the occasion an even more vulgar coat than usual. As for the music, it matched the coat completely. For my dear pupil Katherina Cavalieri he had written quite simply the showiest aria I'd ever heard.

Faintly we hear the whizzing scale passages for Soprano which end the aria "Martern aller Arten"

Ten minutes of scales and ornaments, amounting in sum to a vast emptiness. So ridiculous was the piece in fact—so much what might be demanded by a foolish young soprano—that I knew precisely what Mozart must have demanded in return for it.

The final orchestral chords of the aria. Silence. No-one moves

Although engaged to be married, *he'd had her!* I knew that beyond any doubt. (*Bluntly*) The Creature had had my darling girl.

Loudly we hear the brilliant Turkish finale of Seraglio. There is great applause from those watching. Mozart jumps to his feet and acknowledges it. The Emperor rises—as do all—and gestures graciously to the "stage" in invitation

Katherina Cavalieri runs on downstage in her costume, all plumes and flounces, to renewed cheering and clapping. She curtsies to the Emperor—is kissed by Salieri—presented to his wife—curtsies again to Mozart and, flushed with triumph, moves to one side

In the ensuing brief silence Constanze rushes down from the back, wildly excited. She flings herself on Mozart, not even noticing the Emperor

Constanze Oh, well done, lovey! . . . Well done, pussy-wussy! . . .

Mozart indicates the proximity of His Majesty

Oh! . . . 'Scuse *me*! (*She curtsies in embarrassment*)
Mozart Majesty, may I present my fiancée, Fräulein Weber.
Jospeh *Enchanté, Fräulein.*
Constanze Your Majesty!
Mozart Constanze is a singer herself.

Joseph Indeed?

Constanze (*embarrassed*) I'm not at all, Majesty. Don't be silly, Wolfgang!

Joseph So, Mozart—a good effort. Decidedly that. A good effort.

Mozart Did you really like it, Sire?

Joseph I thought it was most interesting. Yes, indeed. A trifle—how shall one say? (*To Orsini-Rosenberg*) How shall one say, Director?

Orsini-Rosenberg (*subserviently*) Too many notes, Your Majesty?

Joseph Very well put. Too many notes.

Mozart I don't understand.

Joseph My dear fellow, don't take it too hard. There are in fact only so many notes the ear can hear in the course of an evening. I think I'm right in saying that, aren't I, Court Composer?

Salieri (*uncomfortably*) Well yes, I would say yes, on the whole, yes, Majesty.

Joseph There you are. It's clever. It's German. It's quality work. And there are simply too many notes. Do you see?

Mozart There are just as many notes, Majesty, neither more nor less, as are required.

Pause

Joseph Ah . . . Well, there it is.

He goes off abruptly, followed by Orsini-Rosenberg and von Strack. Kapellmeister Bonno, van Swieten and Teresa leave together and the Citizens of Vienna wander off

Mozart (*nervously*) Is he angry?

Salieri Not at all. He respects you for your views.

Mozart (*nervously*) I hope so . . . What did you think yourself, sir? Did you care for the piece at all?

Salieri Yes, of course, Mozart—at its best it is truly charming.

Mozart And at other times?

Salieri (*smoothly*) Well, just occasionally at other times—in Katherina's aria for example—it was a little excessive.

Mozart Katherina is an excessive girl. In fact she's insatiable.

Salieri All the same, as my revered teacher the Chevalier Gluck used to say to me—one must avoid music that smells of music.

Mozart What does that mean?

Salieri Music which makes one aware too much of the virtuosity of the composer.

Mozart Gluck is absurd.

Salieri What do you say?

Mozart He's talked all his life about modernizing opera, but creates people so lofty they sound as though they shit marble.

Constanze gives a little scream of shock

Constanze Oh, 'scuse me! . . .

Mozart (*breaking out*) No, but it's too much! Gluck says! Gluck says!

Chevalier Gluck! . . . What's Chevalier? I'm a Chevalier. The Pope made me a Chevalier when I was still wetting my bed.

Constanze Wolferl!

Mozart Anyway it's ridiculous. Only stupid farts use titles.

Salieri (*blandly*) Such as Court Composer?

Mozart What? . . . (*Realizing*) Ah. Oh. Ha. Ha. Well! . . . My father's right again. He always tells me I should padlock my mouth . . . Actually, I shouldn't speak at all!

Salieri (*soothingly*) Nonsense. I'm just being what the Emperor would call *cattivo*. Won't you introduce me to your charming fiancée?

Mozart Oh, of course! Constanze, this is Herr Court Composer Salieri, Fräulein Weber.

Salieri (*bowing*) Delighted, *cara Fräulein*.

Constanze (*bobbing*) How do you do, Excellency.

Salieri You are the sister of Aloysia Weber, the soprano, are you not?

Constanze I am, Excellency.

Salieri A beauty herself, but you exceed her by far, if I may observe.

Constanze Oh, thank you!

Salieri May I ask when you marry?

Mozart (*nervously*) We have to secure my father's consent. He's an excellent man—a wonderful man—but in some ways a little stubborn.

Salieri Excuse me, but how old are you?

Mozart Twenty-six.

Salieri Then your father's consent is scarcely indispensable.

Constanze (*to Mozart*) You see?

Mozart (*uncomfortably*) Well no, it's not *indispensable*—of course not! . . .

Salieri My advice to you is to marry and be happy. You have found—it's quite obvious—*un tesoro raro*!

Constanze Ta very much.

Salieri kisses Constanze's hand. She is delighted

Salieri Good-night to you both.

Constanze Good-night, Excellency!

Mozart Good-night, sir. And thank you . . . Come, Stanzerl.

Constanze and Mozart depart delightedly

He watches them go

Salieri (*to the Audience*) As I watched her walk away on the arm of the Creature, I felt the lightning thought strike—"Have her! Her for Katherina!" . . . Abomination! . . . Never in my life had I entertained a notion so sinful!

The Lights change: the eighteenth-century theatre fades

The Venticelli come on merrily, as if from some celebration. One holds a bottle; the other a glass. During the following Servants enter and take off the chairs and benches

Venticello 1 They're married.

Salieri (*to them*) What?
Venticello 2 Mozart and Weber—married!
Salieri Really?
Venticello 1 His father will be furious!
Venticello 2 They didn't even wait for his consent!
Salieri Have they set up house?
Venticello 1 Wipplingerstrasse.
Venticello 2 Number twelve.
Venticello 1 Not bad.
Venticello 2 Considering they've no money.
Salieri Is that really true?
Venticello 1 He's wildly extravagant.
Venticello 2 Lives way beyond his means.
Salieri But he has pupils.
Venticello 1 Only three.
Salieri (*to them*) Why so few?
Venticello 1 He's embarrassing.
Venticello 2 Makes scenes.
Venticello 1 Makes enemies.
Venticello 2 Even Strack, whom he cultivates.
Salieri Chamberlain Strack?
Venticello 1 Only last night.
Venticello 2 At Kapellmeister Bonno's.

*   *   *   *

Bonno's House

The Lights change instantly

Mozart comes in with von Strack. He is high on wine, and holding a glass The Venticelli join the scene, but still talk out of it to Salieri. One of them fills Mozart's glass

Mozart Seven months in this city and not one job! I'm not to be tried again, is that it?
Von Strack Of course not.
Mozart I know what goes on,—and so do you. Vienna is completely in the hands of foreigners. Worthless Italians like *Kapellmeister Bonno*!
Von Strack Please! You're in the man's house!
Mozart Court Composer *Salieri*!
Von Strack Hush!
Mozart Did you see his last opera?—*The Chimney Sweep*? . . . Did you?
Von Strack Of course I did.
Mozart Dogshit. Dried dogshit.
Von Strack (*outraged*) I beg your pardon!

Mozart goes to the fortepiano and thumps on it monotonously

Mozart (*singing*) Pom-pom, pom-pom, pom-pom, pom-pom! Tonic and dominant, tonic and dominant from here to resurrection! Not one interesting modulation all night. Salieri is a musical idiot!

Von Strack Please!

Venticello 1 (*to Salieri*) He'd had too much to drink.

Venticello 2 He often has.

Mozart Why are Italians so terrified by the slightest complexity in music? Show them one chromatic passage and they *faint*! . . . "Oh how sick! How morbid!" (*Falsetto*) Morboso! . . . Nervoso! . . . Ohimè! . . . No wonder the music at this court is so dreary.

Count Orsini-Rosenberg enters upstage and is suddenly standing between the Venticelli, listening. He is unobserved by Mozart. He wears a waistcoat of bright green silk, and an expression of supercilious interest

Von Strack Lower your voice.

Mozart Lower your breeches! . . . That's just a joke—just a joke! (*He sees Orsini-Rosenberg. After a pause, pleasantly to him*) You look like a toad . . . I mean you're goggling like a toad. (*He giggles*)

Orsini-Rosenberg (*blandly*) You would do best to retire tonight, for your own sake.

Mozart Salieri has fifty pupils. I have three. How am I to live? I'm a married man now! . . . Of course I realize you don't concern yourself with *money* in these exalted circles. All the same, did you know behind his back His Majesty is known as Kaiser Keep It? (*He giggles wildly*)

Von Strack *Mozart!*

He stops giggling

Mozart I shouldn't have said that, should I? Forgive me. It was just a joke. Another joke! . . . I can't help myself! . . . We're all friends here, aren't we?

Von Strack and Orsini-Rosenberg glare at him

Von Strack leaves abruptly, much offended

Mozart What's wrong with him?

Orsini-Rosenberg Good-night. (*He turns to go*)

Mozart No, no, no—please! (*He grabs the Director's arm*) Your hand please, first!

Unwillingly Orsini-Rosenberg gives him his hand. Mozart kisses it

(*Humbly*) Give me a post, sir.

Orsini-Rosenberg That is not in my power, Mozart.

Mozart The Princess Elizabeth is looking for an instructor. One word from you could secure it for me.

Orsini-Rosenberg I regret that is solely in the recommendation of Court Composer Salieri. (*He disengages himself*)

Mozart Do you know I am better than any musician in Vienna? . . . Do you?

Orsini-Rosenberg leaves

(*Calling after him*) Italians!—I *sick* of them! Italians everywhere . . .!

(*Suddenly he giggles to himself, like a child and starts singing — to the tune of "La Ci Darem la Mano" from* Don Giovanni) The girl who doesn't love me — the girl who doesn't love me — the girl who doesn't love me — can lick my arse instead!

He runs off

Salieri (*watching him go*) Barely one month later, that thought of revenge became more than thought.

Black-out

         *   *   *   *

The Library of the Baroness Waldstädten

Two simultaneous shouts bring up the Lights

In the Light Box against the handsome wallpaper stand three masked figures: Constanze, flanked on either side by the Venticelli. All three are guests at a party, and are playing a game of forfeits

Two Servants stand frozen, holding the large wing-chair between them. Two more hold the big table of sweetmeats

Venticello 1 Forfeit! . . . Forfeit! . . .
Venticello 2 Forfeit, Stanzerl! You've got to forfeit!
Constanze I won't.
Venticello 1 You have to.
Venticello 2 It's the game.

The Servants unfreeze and set down the furniture. Salieri moves to the wing-chair and sits

Salieri (*to the Audience*) Once again — believe it or not — I was in the same concealing chair in the Baroness' library — (*taking the bowl from the little table*) — and consuming the same delicious dessert.
Venticello 1 You lost — now there's the penalty!
Salieri (*to the Audience*) A party celebrating the New Year's Eve. I was on my own — my dear spouse Teresa visiting her parents in Italy.
Constanze Well, *what*? . . . What is it?

Venticello 1 snatches up an old-fashioned round ruler from off the fortepiano

Venticello 1 I want to measure your calves.
Constanze Oooo!
Venticello 1 Well?
Constanze Definitely not! You cheeky bugger!
Venticello 1 Now come on!
Venticello 2 You've got to let him, Stanzerl. All's fair in love and forfeits.
Constanze No it isn't — so you can both buzz off!
Venticello 1 If you don't let me, you won't be allowed to play again.
Constanze Well choose something else.
Venticello 1 I've chosen that. Now get up on the table. Quick, quick! *Allez-oop!* (*Gleefully he shifts the plates of sweetmeats from the table*)
Constanze Quick, then! . . . Before anyone sees!

The two masked men lift the shrieking masked girl up on to the table

Venticello 1 Hold her, Friedrich.
Constanze I don't have to be held, thank you!
Venticello 2 Yes, you do: that's part of the penalty.

Venticello 2 holds her ankles firmly, whilst Venticello 1 thrusts the ruler under her skirts and measures her legs. Excitedly, Salieri puts down the bowl on the small table and reverses his position so that he can kneel in the wing-chair, and watch. Constanze giggles delightedly, then becomes outraged—or pretends to be

Constanze Stop it! ... Stop that! That's quite enough of that! (*She bends down and tries to slap him*)
Venticello 1 Seventeen inches—knee to ankle!
Venticello 2 Let me do it! You hold her.
Constanze That's not fair!
Venticello 2 Yes, it is. You lost to me too.
Constanze It's been done now! Let me *down*!
Venticello 2 Hold her, Karl.
Constanze No! ...

Venticello 1 holds her ankles. Venticello 2 thrusts his head entirely under her skirts. She squeals

No—stop it! ... *No!* ...

In the middle of this undignified scene Mozart comes rushing on—also masked

Mozart (*outraged*) Constanze!

They freeze. Salieri ducks back down and sits hidden in the chair

Gentlemen, if you please.
Constanze It's only a game, Wolferl! ...
Venticello 1 We meant no harm, 'pon my word.
Mozart (*stiffly*) Come down off that table please.

They hand her down

Thank you. We'll see you later.
Venticello 2 Now look, Mozart, don't be pompous——
Mozart Please excuse us now.

The Venticelli go

The little man is very angry. He tears off his mask

(*To Constanze*) Do you realize what you've done?
Constanze No, what? ... (*Flustered, she busies herself restoring the plates of sweetmeats to the table*)
Mozart Just lost your reputation, that's all! You're now a loose girl.
Constanze Don't be so stupid. (*She too removes her mask*)
Mozart You are a married woman, for God's sake!

Constanze And what of it?

Mozart A young wife does not allow her legs to be handled in public. Couldn't you at least have measured your own ugly legs?

Constanze *What?* Of course they're not as good as Aloysia's! My sister had perfect legs, we all know that!

Mozart (*raising his voice*) Do you know what you've done?! ... You've shamed me—that's all! *Shamed* me!

Constanze Oh, don't be so ridiculous!

Mozart Shamed me—in front of *them*!

Constanze (*suddenly furious*) *You*—shamed *you*? ... That's a laugh! If there's any shame around, lovey, it's *mine*!

Mozart What do you mean?

Constanze You've only had every pupil who ever came to you.

Mozart That's not true.

Constanze Every single female pupil!

Mozart Name them! *Name them!*

Constanze The Aurnhammer girl! The Rumbeck girl! Katherina Cavalieri—that sly little whore! *She* wasn't even your pupil—she was Salieri's. Which actually, my dear, may be why he had hundreds and you have none! He doesn't drag them into bed!

Mozart Of course he doesn't! He can't get it up, that's why! ... Have you heard his music? That's the sound of someone who *can't get it up*! At least *I* can do that!

Constanze I'm sick of you!

Mozart (*shouting*) No-one ever said I couldn't do *that*!

Constanze (*bursting into tears*) I don't give a fart! I hate you! I hate you for ever and ever—I hate you! (*A tiny pause. She weeps*)

Mozart (*helplessly*) Oh Stanzerl, don't cry. Please don't cry ... I can't bear it when you cry. I just didn't want you to look cheap in people's eyes, that's all. Here! (*He snatches up the ruler*) Beat me. Beat me ... I'm your slave. Stanzi-marini. Stanzi-marini-bini-gini. I'll just stand here like a little lamb and bear your strokes. Here. Do it ... *Batti.*

Constanze No.

Mozart *Batti, batti. Mio tesoro!*

Constanze No!

Mozart Stanzerly-wanzerly-piggly-poo!

Constanze Stop it.

Mozart Stanzy-wanzy had a fit. Shit her stays and made them split!

She giggles despite herself

Constanze Stop it.

Mozart When they took away her skirt. Stanzy wanzy ate the dirt!

Constanze Stop it now!

She snatches the ruler and gives him a whack with it. He yowls playfully

Mozart Ooooo! Oooo! Oooo! Do it again! Do it again! I cast myself at your stinking feet, Madonna!

He does so. She whacks him some more as he crouches, but always lightly, scarcely looking at him, divided between tears and laughter. Mozart drums his feet with pleasure

Mozart Ow! Ow! Ow!

And then suddenly Salieri, unable to bear another second, cries out involuntarily

Salieri *Ah!!!*

The young couple freezes. Salieri—discovered—hastily converts his noise of disgust into a yawn, and stretches as if waking up from a nap. He peers out of the wing-chair

Good-evening.

Constanze (*embarrassed*) Excellency ...

Mozart How long have you been there?

Salieri I was asleep until a second ago. Are you two quarrelling?

Mozart No, of course not.

Constanze Yes, we are. He's been very irritating.

Salieri (*rising*) *Caro Herr*, tonight is the time for New Year resolutions. Irritating lovely ladies cannot surely be one of yours. May I suggest you bring us each a *sorbetto* from the dining-room?

Mozart But why don't we all go to the table?

Constanze Herr Salieri is quite right. Bring them here—it'll be your punishment.

Mozart Stanzi!

Salieri Come now, I can keep your wife company. There cannot be a better peace offering than a *sorbetto* of aniseed.

Constanze I prefer tangerine.

Salieri Very well, tangerine. (*Greedily*) But if you could possibly manage aniseed for me, I'd be deeply obliged ... So the New Year can begin coolly for all three of us.

A pause. Mozart hesitates—and then bows

Mozart I'm honoured, *Signore*, of course. And then I'll play you at billiards. What do you say?

Salieri I'm afraid I don't play.

Mozart (*with surprise*) You don't?

Constanze Wolferl would rather play at billiards than anything. He's very good at it.

Mozart I'm the best! I may nod occasionally at composing, but at billiards—never!

Salieri A virtuoso of the cue.

Mozart Exactly! It's a virtuoso's game! ... (*He snatches up the ruler and treats it as if it were a cue*) I think I shall write a Grand Fantasia for Billiard Balls! Trillos. Acciaccaturas! Whole arpeggios in ivory! Then I'll play it myself in public! ... It'll have to be *me* because none of those Italian charlatans like Clementi will be able to get his fingers round the cue! *Scusate, Signore!*

He gives a swanky flourish of the hand and struts off

Constanze He's a love, really.

Salieri And lucky, too, in you. You are, if I may so, an astonishing creature.

Constanze Me? . . . Ta very much.

Salieri On the other hand, your husband does not appear to be so thriving.

Constanze (*seizing her opportunity*) We're desperate, sir.

Salieri What?

Constanze We've no money and no prospects of any. That's the truth.

Salieri I don't understand. He gives many public concerts.

Constanze They don't pay enough. What he needs is pupils. Illustrious pupils. His father calls us spendthrifts, but that's unfair. I manage as well as anyone could. There's simply not enough. Don't tell him I talked to you, please.

Salieri (*intimately*) This is solely between us. How can I help?

Constanze My husband needs security, sir. If only he could find regular employment, everything would be all right. Is there nothing at court?

Salieri Not at the moment.

Constanze (*harder*) The Princess Elizabeth needs a tutor.

Salieri Really? I hadn't heard.

Constanze One word from you and the post would be his. Other pupils would follow at once.

Salieri (*looking off*) He's coming back.

Constanze Please . . . please, Excellency. You can't imagine what a difference it would make.

Salieri We can't speak of it now.

Constanze When then? Oh, please!

Salieri Can you come and see me tomorrow? Alone?

Constanze I can't do that.

Salieri I'm a married man.

Constanze All the same.

Salieri When does he work?

Constanze Afternoons.

Salieri Then come at three.

Constanze I can't possibly!

Salieri Yes or no? In his interests?

A pause. She hesitates—opens her mouth—then smiles and abruptly runs off

(*To the Audience*) So I'd done it. Spoken aloud. Invited her! What of that vow made in church? Fidelity—virtue—all of that? . . . What did she think of me—this careful Italian? Sincere friend or hopeful seducer? . . . Would she come? . . . I had no idea!

Servants enter and remove the wing-chair and large sweetmeat table. Others come on and replace it with two small gilded chairs which they put C, facing out front, quite close together. Others again surreptitiously bring in the old dressing-robe and shawl which Salieri discarded before and leave them on the fortepiano. When this is completed they exit

*   *   *   *

Salieri's Apartments

The curtains of the Light Box descend and again images of long windows are projected on to them

Salieri If she did, how would I behave? I had no idea of that either . . . Next afternoon I waited in a fever! Was I actually going to seduce a young wife of two months' standing . . . Part of me—much of me—wanted it, badly. Badly. Yes, badly was the word! . . .

The clock strikes three. On the first stroke the bell sounds. He rises excitedly

There she was! On the stroke! She'd come . . . She'd *come*!

The Cook, still as fat but forty years younger, enters L. He proudly carries a plate piled with brandied chestnuts

Salieri takes the plate from him nervously, nodding with approval, and sets them on the little table

(*To the Cook*) Grazie. Grazie tanti . . . Via, via, via!

The Cook bows as Salieri dismisses him and goes out the same way, smirking suggestively

The Valet comes in R—he is also forty years younger—and behind him Constanze, wearing a pretty hat and carrying a portfolio

Signora!
Constanze (*curtsying*) Excellency.
Salieri Benvenuta. (*To the Valet in dismissal*) Grazie.

The Valet goes

Well. You have come.
Constanze I should not have done. My husband would be frantic if he knew. He's a very jealous man.
Salieri Are you a jealous woman?
Constanze Why do you ask?
Salieri It's not a passion I understand . . . You're looking even prettier than you were last night, if I may say so.
Constanze Ta very much! . . . I brought you some manuscripts by Wolfgang. When you see them you'll undertand how right he is for a royal appointment. Will you look at them, please, while I wait?
Salieri You mean now?
Constanze Yes, I have to take them back with me. He'll miss them otherwise. He doesn't make copies. These are all the originals.
Salieri Sit down. Let me offer you something special.
Constanze (*sitting*) What's that?
Salieri (*producing the plate*) Capezzoli di Venere. Nipples of Venus. Roman chestnuts in brandied sugar.
Constanze No, thank you.
Salieri Do try. They were made especially for you.
Constanze Me?

Salieri Yes. They're quite rare.

Constanze Well then, I'd better hadn't I? Just one ... Ta very much. (*She takes one and puts it in her mouth. The taste amazes her*) Oh! ... Oh! ... Oh! ... They're *delish*!

Salieri (*lustfully watching her eat*) Aren't they?

Constanze Mmmmm!

Salieri Have another.

Constanze (*taking two more*) I couldn't possibly.

Carefully he moves round behind her, and seats himself on the chair next to her

Salieri I think you're the most generous girl in the world.

Constanze Generous?

Salieri It's my word for you. I thought last night that Constanze is altogether too stiff a name for that girl. I shall rechristen her "Generosa". *La Generosa*. Then I'll write a glorious song for her under that title and she'll sing it, just for me.

Constanze (*smiling*) I am much out of practice, sir.

Salieri *La Generosa*. (*He leans a little towards her*) Don't tell me it's going to prove inaccurate, my name for you.

Constanze (*coolly*) What name do you give your wife, Excellency?

Salieri (*equally coolly*) I'm not an excellency, and I call my wife Signora Salieri. If I named her anything else it would be *La Statua*. She's a very upright lady.

Constanze Is she here now? I'd like to meet her.

Salieri Alas, no. At the moment she's visiting her mother in Verona.

She starts very slightly out of her chair. Salieri gently restrains her

Constanze: tomorrow evening I dine with the Emperor. One word from me recommending your husband as tutor to the Princess Elizabeth, and that invaluable post is his. Believe me, when I speak to His Majesty in matters musical, no-one contradicts me.

Constanze I believe you.

Salieri *Bene*. (*Still sitting, he takes his* mouchoir *and delicately wipes her mouth with it*) Surely service of that sort deserves a little recompense in return?

Constanze How little?

Slight pause

Salieri The size of a kiss.

Slight pause

Constanze Just one?

Slight pause

Salieri If one seems fair to you.

She looks at him—then kisses him lightly on the mouth. Longer pause

Does it?

She gives him a longer kiss. He makes to touch her with his hand. She breaks off

Constanze I fancy that's fairness enough.

Pause

Salieri (*carefully*) A pity ... It's somewhat small pay, to secure a post every musician in Vienna is hoping for.
Constanze What do you mean?
Salieri Is it not clear?
Constanze No. Not at all.
Salieri Another pity ... A thousand pities.

Pause

Constanze I don't believe it ... I just don't believe it!
Salieri What?
Constanze What you've just said.
Salieri (*hastily*) I said nothing. What did I say?

Constanze gets up and Salieri rises in panic

Constanze Oh, I'm going! ... I'm getting out of this!
Salieri Constanze ...
Constanze Let me pass, please.
Salieri Constanze, listen to me! I'm a clumsy man. You think me sophisticated—I'm not at all. Take a true look. I've no cunning. I live on ink and sweetmeats. I never see women at all ... When I met you last night, I envied Mozart from the depths of my soul. Out of that envy came stupid thoughts. For one silly second I dared imagine that—out of the vast store you obviously possess—you might spare me one coin of tenderness your rich husband does not need—and inspire me also.

Pause. She laughs

I amuse.
Constanze Mozart was right. You're wicked.
Salieri He said that?
Constanze "All Italians are performers," he said. "Be careful with that one." Meaning you. He was being comic of course.
Salieri Yes. (*Abruptly he turns his back on her*)
Constanze But not that comic, actually. I mean you're acting a pretty obvious role aren't you, dear? A small town boy, and all the time as clever as cutlets! ... (*Mock tender*) Ah!—you are sulking? *Are* you? ... When Mozart sulks I smack his botty. He rather likes it. Do you want me to scold you a bit and smack your botty too?

She hits him lightly with the portfolio. He turns in a fury

Salieri How dare you?! ... *You silly, common girl!*

A dreadful silence

(*Icily*) Forgive me. Let us confine our talk to your husband. He is a brilliant keyboard player, no question. However the Princess Elizabeth also requires a tutor in vocal music. I am not convinced he is the man for that. I would like to look at the pieces you've brought, and decide if he is mature enough. I will study them overnight—and you will study my proposal. Not to be vague: that is the price.

He extends his hand for the portfolio, and she surrenders it

Good-afternoon. (*He turns from her and places the portfolio on a chair*)

Constanze lingers, tries to speak—cannot—and goes out quickly

*   *   *   *

The Same

Salieri turns in a ferment to the Audience

Salieri Fiasco! ... Fiasco! ... The sordidness of it! The sheer sweating sordidness! ... Worse than if I'd actually done it! ... To be that much in sin and feel so *ridiculous* as well! There was no excuse. If now my music was rejected by God forever, it was my fault, mine alone. Would she return tomorrow? Never. And if she did, what then? What would I do? ... Apologize profoundly—or try again? ... (*Crying out*) *Nobile, nobile Salieri!* ... What had he done to me—this Mozart! Before he came did I behave like this? Did I? Toy with adultery? Blackmail women? Twist myself into cruelties? It was all going!—slipping!—growing *rotten*—because of *him*! (*He moves upstage in a fever—reaches out to take the portfolio on the chair—but as if fearful of what he might find inside it he withdraws his hand and sits instead. A pause. He contemplates the music lying there as if it were a great confection he is dying to eat, but dare not. Then suddenly he snatches at it—tears the ribbon—opens the case and stares greedily at the manuscripts within*)

Music sounds instantly, faintly, in the theatre, as his eye falls on the first page. It is the opening of the Twenty-Ninth Symphony, in A Major

(*Over the music, reading the manuscript*) She had said that these were his original scores. First and only drafts of the music. Yet they looked like fair copies. They showed no corrections of any kind.

He looks up from the manuscript at the Audience: the music abruptly stops

It was puzzling—then suddenly alarming. What was evident was that Mozart was simply transcribing music——

He resumes looking at the music. Immediately the Sinfonia Concertante for Violin and Viola *sounds faintly*

—completely finished in his head. And finished as most music is never finished.

He looks up again: the music breaks off

Displace one note and there would be diminishment. Displace one phrase and the structure would fall.

He resumes reading, and the music also resumes: a ravishing phrase from the slow movement of the Concerto for Flute and Harp

Here again—only now in abundance—were the same sounds I'd heard in the library. The same crushed harmonies—glancing collisions—agonizing delights.

And he looks up: again the music stops

The truth was clear. That Serenade had been no accident.

Very low, in the theatre, a faint thundery sound is heard accumulating, like a distant sea

I was staring through the cage of those meticulous ink strokes at an Absolute Beauty!

And out of the thundery roar writhes and rises the clear sound of a Soprano, singing the "Kyrie" from the C Minor Mass. *The accretion of noise around her voice falls away—it is suddenly clear and bright—then clearer and brighter. The light grows bright: too bright: burning white, then scalding white! Salieri rises in the downpour of it, and in the flood of the music which is growing even louder—filling the theatre—as the Soprano yields to the full Chorus, fortissimo, singing its massive counterpoint*

This is by far the loudest sound the Audience has yet heard. Salieri staggers towards us, holding the manuscripts in his hand, like a man caught in a tumbling and violent sea

Finally the drums crash in below: Salieri drops the portfolio of manuscripts— and falls senseless to the ground. At the same second the music explodes into a long, echoing, distorted boom, signifying some dreadful annihilation. The sound remains suspended over the prone figure in a menacing continuum—no longer music at all. Then it dies away, and there is only silence

The Lights fade

A long pause. Salieri is quite still, his head by the pile of manuscripts

Finally the clock sounds: eight times. Salieri stirs as it does. Slowly he raises his head and looks up. And now—quietly at first—he addresses his God

Capisco! I know my fate. Now for the first time I feel my emptiness as Adam felt his nakedness . . . (*Slowly he rises to his feet*) Tonight at an inn somewhere in this city stands a giggling child who can put on paper, without actually setting down his billiard cue, casual notes which turn my most considered ones into lifeless scratches. *Grazie Signore!* You gave me the desire to serve You—which most men do not have—then saw to it the service was shameful in the ears of the server. *Grazie!* You gave me the desire to praise You—which most do not feel—then made me mute. *Grazie tanti!* You put into me perception of the Incomparable—which most men never know!—then ensured that I would know myself forever mediocre. (*His voice gains power*) *Why? ... What is my fault? ...* Until this day I have pursued virtue with rigour. I have laboured long hours to relieve my fellow men. I have worked and worked the talent You allowed me. (*Calling up*) *You know how hard I've worked!*—Solely that in the end, in the practice of the art which alone makes the world comprehensible to me, I might hear Your Voice! And now I do hear it and it says only one name: MOZART! ... Spiteful, sniggering, conceited, infantine Mozart!— who has never worked one minute to help another man!—shit-talking Mozart with his botty-smacking wife!—*him* You have chosen to be your sole conduct! And *my* only reward—my sublime privilege—is to be the sole man alive in this time who shall clearly recognize Your Incarnation! (*Savagely*) *Grazie e grazie ancora!* (*After a pause*) So be it! From this time we are enemies, You and I! I'll not accept it from You—*Do you hear? ...* They say God is not mocked. I tell you, *Man* is not mocked! ... *I* am not mocked! ... They say the spirit bloweth where it listeth: I tell you NO! It must list to virtue or not blow at all! (*Yelling*) *Dio Ingiusto!*—You are the Enemy! I name Thee now—*Nemico Eterno!* And this I swear. To my last breath I shall *block* You on earth, as far as I am able! (*He glares up at God. To the Audience*) What use, after all, is Man, if not to teach God His lessons? (*Pause. Suddenly he speaks again to us in the voice of an old man*) And now——

He slips off his powdered wig, crosses to the fortepiano and takes from its lid the old dressing-robe and shawl which he discarded when he conducted us back to the eighteenth century. These he slips on over his court coat. It is again 1823

—before I tell you what happened next—God's answer to me—and indeed Constanze's—and all the horrors that followed—let me stop. The bladder, being a human appendage, is not something you ghosts need concern yourselves with yet. I being alive, though barely, am at its constant call. It is now one hour before dawn—when I must dismiss us both. When I return I'll tell you about the war I fought with God through His preferred Creature—Mozart, named *Amadeus*. In the waging of which, of course, the Creature had to be destroyed.

He bows to the Audience with malignant slyness—snatches a pastry from the stand—and leaves the stage, chewing at it voraciously. The manuscripts lie where he spilled them in his fall

The House Lights come up as he goes

ACT II

Salieri's Apartments. November 1823. Early morning

The House Lights go down as Salieri returns

Salieri I have been listening to the cats in the courtyard. They are all singing Rossini. It is obvious that cats have declined as badly as composers. Domenico Scarlatti owned one which would actually stroll across the keyboard and pick out passable subjects for fugue. But that was a Spanish cat of the Enlightenment. It appreciated counterpoint. Nowadays all cats appreciate is coloratura. Like the rest of the public.

He comes downstage and addresses the Audience directly

This is now the very last hour of my life. You must understand me. Not forgive. I do not seek forgiveness. I was a good man, as the world calls good. *What use was it to me?* Goodness could not make me a good composer. Was Mozart good? . . . Goodness is nothing in the furnace of art.

Pause

On that dreadful Night of the Manuscripts my life acquired a terrible and thrilling purpose. The blocking of God in one of His purest manifestations. I had the power. God needed Mozart to let Himself into the world. And Mozart needed *me* to get him worldly advancement. So it would be a battle to the end—and Mozart was the battleground.

Pause

One thing I knew of Him. God was a cunning Enemy. Witness the fact that in blocking Him in the world I was also given the satisfaction of obstructing a disliked human rival. I wonder which of you will refuse that chance if it is offered.

He regards the Audience maliciously, taking off his dressing-robe and shawl

I felt the danger at once, as soon as I'd uttered my challenge. How would He answer? Would He strike me dead for my impiety? Don't laugh. I was not a sophisticate of the salons. I was a small town Catholic, full of dread!

He puts on his powdered wig, and speaks again in his younger voice. We are back in the eighteenth century

The first thing that happened—suddenly Constanze was back! At ten o'clock at night!

The doorbell sounds

Constanze comes in followed by a helpless Valet

(*In surprise*) Signora!

Constanze (*stiffly*) My husband is at a soirée of Baron van Swieten. A concert of Sebastian Bach. He didn't think I would enjoy it.

Salieri I see. (*Curtly, to the goggling Valet*) I'll ring if we require anything. Thank you.

The Valet goes out

Slight pause

Constanze (*flatly*) Where do we go, then?

Salieri What?

Constanze Do we do it in here? ... Why not? (*She sits, still wearing her hat, in one of the little gilded upright chairs. Deliberately she loosens the strings of her bodice, so that one can just see the tops of her breasts, hitches up her silk skirts above the knees, so that one can also just see the flesh above the tops of the stockings, spreads her legs and regards him with an open stare. Speaking softly*) Well? ... Let's get on with it.

For a second Salieri returns the stare, then looks suddenly away

Salieri (*stiffly*) Your manuscripts are there. Please take them and go. Now. At once.

Pause

Constanze You shit. (*She jumps up and snatches the portfolio*)

Salieri *Via! Don't return!*

Constanze You rotten shit!

Suddenly she runs at him—trying furiously to hit at his face. He grabs her arms, shakes her violently, and hurls her on the floor

Salieri *Via!*

She freezes, staring up at him in hate

(*Calling to the Audience*) You see how it was! I would have liked her—oh yes, just then more than ever! But now I wanted nothing petty! ... My quarrel wasn't with Mozart—it was through him! Through him to God who loved him so. (*Scornfully*) Amadeus! ... Amadeus! ...

Constance picks herself up and runs from the room

Pause. He calms himself, going to the table and selecting a Nipple of Venus to eat

The next day, when Katherina Cavalieri came for her lesson, I made the same halting speech about "coins of tenderness"—and I dubbed the girl *la Generosa*. I regret that my invention in love, as in art, has always been limited. Fortunately Katherina found it sufficient. She consumed twenty Nipples of Venus—kissed me with brandied breath—and slipped easily into my bed.

Katherina comes in languidly, half-dressed, as if from his bedroom

Salieri embraces her, and helps slyly to adjust her peignoir

She remained there as my mistress for many years behind my good wife's back—and I soon erased in sweat the sense of his little body, the Creature's, preceding me.

The girl gives him a radiant smile, and ambles off

So much for my vow of sexual virtue. (*After a slight pause*) The same evening I went to the Palace and resigned from all my committees to help the lot of poor musicans. So much for my vow of social virtue.

The Lights change and the curtains of the Light Box rise and part

Two Servants come on and remove the two gilded chairs

The Emperor enters the Light Box and takes up his position before the vast fireplace, between the golden mirrors

(*Moving upstage*) Then I went to the Emperor and recommended a man of no talent whatever to instruct the Princess Elizabeth.

*   *   *   *

The Palace of Schönbrunn

Joseph Herr Sommer. A dull man, surely? What of Mozart?

Salieri Majesty, I cannot with a clear conscience recommend Mozart to teach royalty. One hears too many stories.

Joseph They may be just gossip.

Salieri One of them I regret relates to a protégée of my own. A very young singer.

Joseph *Charmant!*

Salieri Not pleasant, Majesty, but true.

Joseph I see . . . Let it be Herr Sommer, then. (*He walks down on to the main stage*) I daresay he can't do much harm. To be frank, no-one can do much harm musically to the Princess Elizabeth. (*He strolls away* DL)

Salieri moves DR

Mozart enters DL. *He wears a more natural-looking wig from now on: one indeed intended to represent his own hair of light chestnut, full and gathered at the back with ribbon*

Salieri (*to the Audience*) Mozart certainly did not suspect me. The Emperor announced the appointment in his usual way——

Joseph (*pausing*) Well, there it is.

Joseph goes off

Salieri —and I commiserated with the loser.

Mozart turns and stares bleakly out front. Salieri goes and shakes his hand

Mozart (*bitterly*) It's my own fault. My father always writes, I should be more obedient. *Know my place!* ... He'll send me sixteen lectures when he hears of this! (*He goes slowly up to the fortepiano*)

The Lights lower

Salieri (*watching him; to the audience*) It was a most serious loss as far as Mozart was concerned.

*   *   *   *

Vienna and Glimpses of Opera Houses

The Venticelli glide on

Venticello 1 His list of pupils hardly moves.
Venticello 2 Six at most.
Venticello 1 And now a child to keep!
Venticello 2 A boy.
Salieri Poor fellow. (*To the Audience*) I by contrast prospered. This is the extraordinary truth. If I had expected anger from God—none came. *None!* ... Instead—incredibly—in 'eighty-four and 'eighty-five I came to be regarded as infinitely the superior composer. And this despite the fact that these were the two years in which Mozart wrote his best keyboard concerti and his String Quartets.

The Venticelli stand on either side of Salieri. Mozart sits at the fortepiano

Venticello 1 Haydn calls the Quartets unsurpassed.
Salieri They were—but no-one heard them.
Venticello 2 Van Swieten calls the concerti sublime.
Salieri They were, but no-one noticed.

Mozart plays and conducts from the keyboard. Faintly we hear the Rondo from the Piano Concerto in A Major, K488

> *During the following the Citizens unobtrusively enter the Light Box and take up their positions*

> (*Over the music*) The Viennese greeted each unique concerto with the squeals of pleasure they usually reserved for a new style of bonnet. Each was played once—then totally forgotten! ... I alone was empowered to recognize them fully for what they were: the most perfect things made by man in the whole of the eighteenth century. By contrast, my operas were played everywhere and saluted by everyone! I composed my *Semiramide* for Munich.
Venticello 1 Rapturously received!
Venticello 2 People *faint* with pleasure!

In the Light Box is seen the interior of a brilliantly coloured Opera House, and a stage audience standing up applauding vigorously. Salieri, flanked by the Venticelli, turns upstage and bows to it. The Concerto can scarcely be heard through the din

Salieri I wrote a comic opera for Vienna. *La Grotta di Trofonio*.
Venticello 1 The talk of the city!
Venticello 2 The cafés are buzzing!

Another Opera House interior is lit up. Another stage audience claps vigorously. Again Salieri bows to it

Salieri (*to the Audience*) I finally finished my tragic opera *Danaius*, and produced it in Paris.
Venticello 1 Stupendous reception!
Venticello 2 The plaudits shake the roof!
Venticello 1 Your name sounds throughout the Empire!
Venticello 2 Throughout all Europe!

Yet another Opera House and another excited stage audience is lit up. Salieri bows a third time. Even the Venticelli now applaud him

The Concerto stops

> *Mozart rises from the keyboard and, whilst Salieri speaks, crosses directly through the scene and exits*

Salieri (*to the Audience*) It was incomprehensible. Almost as if I were being pushed deliberately from triumph to triumph! ... I filled my head with golden opinions—yes, and this house with golden furniture!

> *The Citizens exit*

*   *   *   *

Salieri's Apartments

The stage turns gold

> *Servants come on carrying golden chairs upholstered in golden brocade. They place these all over the wooden floor and then exit*

> *The Valet, a little older, appears, divests Salieri of his sky-blue coat and clothes him instead in a frock coat of gold satin. He takes away the old coat*

> *The Cook—also of course a little older—brings on a golden cake-stand piled with more elaborate cakes and, placing this on the little table, takes away the other cake-stand and plate of brandied chestnuts*

Salieri My own taste was for plain things—but I *denied* it! ... I grew confident. I grew resplendent. I gave salons and soirées, and worshipped the season round at the altar of sophistication!

He sits at ease in his salon. The Venticelli sit with him, one on either side

Venticello 1 Mozart heard your comedy last night.
Venticello 2 He spoke of it to the Princess Lichnowsky.
Venticello 1 He said you should be made to clean up your own mess.
Salieri (*taking snuff*) *Really?* What charmers these Salzburgers are!
Venticello 2 People are outraged, by him.

Venticello 1 He empties drawing-rooms. Now van Swieten is angry with him.
Salieri Lord Fugue? I thought he was the Baron's little pet.
Venticello 2 Mozart has asked leave to write an Italian opera.
Salieri (*briskly aside to the Audience*) *Italian Opera! Threat! My kingdom!*
Venticello 1 And the Baron is scandalized.
Salieri But why? What's the theme of it?

Van Swieten comes on quickly from upstage

Van Swieten *Figaro! ... The Marriage of Figaro!* That disgraceful play of Beaumarchais!

The Venticelli slip away at a discreet sign of dismissal from Salieri

Van Swieten joins Salieri and sits on one of the golden chairs

(*To Salieri*) That's all he can find to waste his talent on: a vulgar farce. When I reproved him, he said I reminded him of his father! Noblemen lusting after chambermaids! Their wives dressing up in stupid disguises anyone could penetrate in a second! ... Why set such rubbish to music?

Mozart enters quickly from upstage, accompanied by von Strack. They join Salieri and van Swieten

Mozart Because I want to do a piece about real people, Baron! And I want to set it in a real place! A *boudoir!*—because that to me is the most exciting place on earth! Underclothes on the floor! Sheets still warm from a woman's body! Even a pisspot brimming under the bed!
Van Swieten (*outraged*) Mozart!
Mozart I want life, Baron. Not boring legends!
Von Strack Herr Salieri's recent *Danaius* was a legend and that did not bore the French.
Mozart It is impossible to bore the French—except with real life!
Van Swieten I had assumed, now that you had joined our Brotherhood of Masons, you would choose more elevated themes.
Mozart (*impatiently*) Oh elevated! Elevated! ... The only thing a man should elevate is his doodle.
Van Swieten You are provoking, sir! Has everything to be a joke with you?
Mozart (*desperate*) Excuse language, Baron, but really! How can we go on forever with these gods and heroes?
Van Swieten (*passionately*) Because they *go* on forever—that's why! They represent the eternal in us. Opera is here to ennoble us, Mozart—you and me just as well as the Emperor. It is an aggrandizing art! It celebrates the eternal in man and ignores the ephemeral. The goddess in woman and not the laundress.
Von Strack Well said, sir. Exactly!
Mozart (*imitating his drawl*) Oh well said, yes, well said! Exactly! (*To all of them*) I don't understand you! You're all up on perches, but it doesn't hide your arseholes! You don't give a shit about gods and heroes! If you are honest—each one of you—which of you isn't more at home with his hairdresser than Hercules? Or Horatius? (*To Salieri*) Or your stupid

Danaius, come to that! Or mine—*mine! Mitridate, King of Pontus! Idomeneo, King of Crete!* All those anguished antiques! They're all bores! Bores, bores, bores! (*Suddenly he springs up and jumps on to a chair, like an orator. Declaring it*) All serious operas written this century are boring!

They turn and look at him in shocked amazement. A pause. He gives his little giggle, and then jumps up and down on the chair

Look at us! Four gaping mouths. What a perfect quartet! I'd love to write it—just this second of time, this *now*, as you are! Herr Chamberlain thinking: "Impertinent Mozart. I must speak to the Emperor at once!" Herr Prefect thinking: "Ignorant Mozart. Debasing opera with his vulgarity!" Herr Court Composer thinking: "German Mozart. What can he finally know about music?" And Herr Mozart himself, in the middle, thinking: "I'm just a good fellow. Why do they all disapprove of me?" (*Excitedly, to van Swieten*) That's why opera is important, Baron. Because it's realer than any play! A dramatic poet would have to put all those thoughts down one after another to represent this second of time. The composer can put them all down at once—and still make us hear each one of them. Astonishing device: a vocal quartet! (*More and more excited*) I tell you I want to write a finale lasting half an hour! A quartet becoming a quintet becoming a sextet. On and on, wider and wider—all sounds multiplying and rising together—and the together making a sound entirely new! ... I bet you that's how God hears the world. Millions of sounds ascending at once and mixing in His ear to become an unending music, unimaginable to us! (*To Salieri*) That's our job! That's our job, we composers: combining the inner minds of him and him and him, and her and her—the thoughts of chambermaids and court composers—and turn the audience into God.

Pause. Salieri stares at him fascinated. Embarrassed, Mozart blows a raspberry and giggles

I'm sorry. I talk nonsense all day: it's incurable—ask Stanzerl. (*To van Swieten*) My tongue is stupid. My heart isn't.

Van Swieten No. You're a good fellow under all your nonsense: I know that. He'll make a fine new brother mason, won't he, Salieri?

Salieri Better than I, Baron.

Van Swieten Just try, my friend, to be more serious with your gifts. (*He smiles and presses Mozart's hand*)

Van Swieten goes out

Salieri (*rising*) *Buona fortuna*, Mozart.

Mozart *Grazie, Signore*. (*Rounding on von Strack*) Stop frowning, Herr Chamberlain. I'm a jackass. It's easy to be friends with a jackass: just shake his "hoof".

He forms his hand into a "hoof". Warily von Strack takes it—then springs back as Mozart brays loudly like a donkey

Mozart *Hee-haw!* ... Tell the Emperor the opera's finished.

Von Strack Finished?
Mozart Right here in my noddle. The rest's just scribbling. Goodbye.
Von Strack Good-day to you.
Mozart He's going to be proud of me. You'll see.

Mozart gives a flourish of his hand and goes out, delighted with himself

Von Strack That young man really is . . .
Salieri (*blandly*) Very lively.
Von Strack (*exploding*) Intolerable! . . . *Intolerable!*

Von Strack freezes in a posture of indignation

Salieri (*to the Audience*) How could I stop it? . . . How could I block this
opera of *Figaro*? . . . Incredible to hear, within six weeks! . . .

Orsini-Rosenberg bustles in

Orsini-Rosenberg *Figaro* is complete! The first performance will be on May
the first!
Salieri So soon?
Orsini-Rosenberg There's no way we can stop it!

A slight pause

Salieri (*slyly*) I have an idea. *Una piccola idea!*
Orsini-Rosenberg What?
Salieri *Mi ha detto che un balletto nel terzo atto?*
Orsini-Rosenberg (*puzzled*) *Si.*
Von Strack What does he say?
Salieri *E dimmi— non è vero che l'Imperatore ha probito il balletto nelle sue
opere?*
Orsini-Rosenberg (*realizing*) *Uno balletto* . . . Ah!
Salieri *Precisamente.*
Orsini-Rosenberg Oh, *capisco! Ma che meraviglia! Perfetto?* (*He laughs in
delight*) *Veramente ingegnoso!*
Von Strack (*irritated*) What is it? What is he suggesting?
Salieri See him at the theatre.
Orsini-Rosenberg Of course. Immediately. I'd forgotten. You are brilliant,
Court Composer.
Salieri I? . . . I have said nothing. (*He moves away upstage*)

The dim Lights begin to change, dimming down

Von Strack (*very cross*) I must tell you that I resent this extremely. Mozart
is right in some things. There is far too much Italian *chittero-chattero* at
this court! Now please to inform me at once, what was just said?
Orsini-Rosenberg (*lightly*) *Pazienza*, my dear Chamberlain. *Pazienza*. Just
wait and see!

*From upstage, Salieri beckons to von Strack. Baffled and cross, the Chamber-
lain joins him. They watch together, unseen*

The Lights dim further

*   *   *   *

An Unlit Theatre

The Light Box background shows a projection of lamps glowing faintly in the darkened auditorium. Orsini-Rosenberg sits on one of the golden chairs, C

> *Mozart comes in quickly* R, *wearing another bright coat, and carrying the score of* Figaro. *He crosses to the fortepiano*

Orsini-Rosenberg Mozart ... *Mozart!*
Mozart Yes, Herr Director.
Orsini-Rosenberg (*agreeably*) A word with you, please. Right away.
Mozart Certainly. What is it?
Orsini-Rosenberg I would like to see your score of *Figaro*.
Mozart Oh yes. Why?
Orsini-Rosenberg Just bring it here to me. (*Unmoving*) Into my hand, please.

Mozart hands it to him puzzled. Orsini-Rosenberg turns the pages

> Now tell me: did you not know that His Majesty has expressly forbidden ballet in his operas?

Mozart Ballet?
Orsini-Rosenberg Such as occurs in your third act.
Mozart That is not a ballet, Herr Director. That is a dance at Figaro's wedding.
Orsini-Rosenberg Exactly. A dance.
Mozart (*trying to control himself*) But, the Emperor doesn't mean to prohibit dancing when it's part of the story. He made that law to prevent *insertions* of stupid ballet like in French operas, and quite right too.
Orsini-Rosenberg (*raising his voice*) It is not for you, Herr Mozart, to interpret the Emperor's edicts. Merely to obey them. (*He seizes the offending pages between his fingers*)
Mozart What are you doing? ... What are you doing, Excellency?
Orsini-Rosenberg Taking out what should never have been put in.

In a terrible silence Orsini-Rosenberg tears out the pages, Mozart watches in disbelief. Upstage, Salieri and von Strack look on together from the dimness

> Now, sir, perhaps in future you will obey Imperial commands. (*He tears out some more pages*)

Mozart But ... But—if all that goes—there'll be a hole right at the climax of the story! ... (*Crying out suddenly*) Salieri! *This is Salieri's idea!*
Orsini-Rosenberg Don't be absurd.
Salieri (*to the Audience*) How did he think of that? Nothing I had ever done could possibly make him think of that on his own. Had God given him the idea?!
Mozart It's a conspiracy. I can smell it. I can smell it!
Orsini-Rosenberg Control yourself!
Mozart (*howling*) *But what do you expect me to do?* The first performance is two days off!
Orsini-Rosenberg Write it over. That's your forte, is it not?—writing at speed.

Mozart Not when the music's *perfect*! Not when its absolutely perfect as it is! ..... (*Wildly*) I shall appeal to the Emperor! I'll go to him myself! I'll hold a rehearsal especially for him.

Orsini-Rosenberg The Emperor does not attend rehearsals.

Mozart He'll attend this one. Make no mistake—he'll come to this one! Then he'll deal with *you*!

Orsini-Rosenberg This issue is simple. Write your Act again today—or withdraw the opera. That's final.

Pause. He hands back the mutilated score to its composer. Mozart is shaking

Mozart You shit-pot.

Orsini-Rosenberg, taking the torn papers, turns and walks imperturbably away from him

Foppy, wet-arsed, Italian-loving shit-pot!

Serenely, Orsini-Rosenberg leaves the stage

(*Screeching after him*) Count Orsini-Rosenshit! ... Rosencunt! ... Rosenbugger! ... I'll hold a rehearsal! You'll see! The Emperor will come! You'll see! You'll see! ... *You'll see!!* (*He throws down his score in a storm of hysterical rage*)

Von Strack goes out upstage in the dimness

Salieri ventures down towards the shrieking little man. Mozart suddenly becomes aware of him. He turns, his hand shooting out in an involuntary gesture of accusation

(*To Salieri*) I am *forbidden*! ... I am—forbidden! ... But of course you know already!

Salieri (*quietly*) Know what?

Mozart flings away from him

Mozart (*bitterly*) No matter!

Salieri (*always blandly*) Mozart, permit me. If you wish, I will speak to the Emperor myself. Ask him to attend a rehearsal.

Mozart (*amazed*) You wouldn't.

Salieri I cannot promise he will come—but I can try.

Mozart Sir!

Salieri Good-day. (*He puts up his hands, barring further intimacy*)

Mozart retreats to the fortepiano

(*To the Audience*) Needless to say I did nothing whatever in the matter. Yet—to my total stupefaction——

Von Strack and Orsini-Rosenberg hurry on downstage

—in the middle of the last rehearsal of *Figaro* next day ...

The Emperor Joseph comes on from upstage

Joseph (*cheerfully*) Fêtes and fireworks! Fêtes and fireworks! Gentlemen, good-afternoon!

*   *   *   *

The Theatre

Salieri (*to the Audience*) Entirely against his usual practice, the Emperor appeared!

Von Strack and Orsini-Rosenberg look at each other in consternation. Joseph seats himself excitedly on one of the golden chairs, facing out front. As with the premiere of Seraglio *seen in Act I, he watches the Audience as if it were the opera*

Joseph I can't wait for this, Mozart, I assure you! *Je prévois des merveilles!*
Mozart (*bowing fervently*) Majesty!

The Courtiers sit also: von Strack on his right-hand side, Orsini-Rosenberg on his left. Salieri also sits, near the keyboard

Salieri (*to the Audience*) What did this mean? Was this proof God had finally decided to defend Mozart against me? Was He engaging with me at last?

Mozart passes behind Salieri

Mozart (*earnestly, sotto voce*) I am so grateful to you, I cannot express it!
Salieri (*aside, to him*) Hush. Say nothing.

Mozart goes on quickly to the fortepiano and sits at it

   (*To the Audience*) One thing about the event certainly seemed more than coincidence.

Music sounds faintly: the end of the third act of Figaro, *just before the dance music starts*

   Strangely, His Majesty had arrived at precisely the moment when the dancers would have begun, (*after a pause*) had not they and their music been entirely cut.

The music stops abruptly

   He and all of us watched the action proceed in total silence.

Flanked by his courtiers, the Emperor stares out front, following with his eyes what is obviously a silent pantomime. His face expresses bewilderment. Orsini-Rosenberg watches his sovereign anxiously. Finally the monarch speaks

Joseph I don't understand. Is it modern?
Mozart (*jumping up nervously from the keyboard*) No, Majesty.
Joseph Then what?
Mozart The Herr Director has removed a dance that would have occurred at this point.
Joseph (*to Orsini-Rosenberg*) Why was this done?
Orsini-Rosenberg It's your own regulation, Sire. No ballet in your opera.
Mozart Majesty, this is not a ballet. It is part of a wedding feast: entirely necessary for the story.
Joseph Well, it certainly looks very odd the way it is. I can't say I like it.
Mozart Nor do I, Majesty.

Joseph Do you like it, Rosenberg?

Orsini-Rosenberg It's not a question of liking, Majesty. Your own law decrees it.

Joseph Yes. All the same, this is nonsense. Look at them: they're like waxworks up there.

Orsini-Rosenberg Well, not exactly, Majesty.

Joseph I don't like waxworks.

Mozart Nor do I, Majesty.

Joseph Well, who would? What do you say, Salieri?

Salieri Italians are fond of waxworks, Majesty. (*After a pause*) Our religion is largely based upon them.

Joseph You are *cattivo* again, Court Composer.

Von Strack (*intervening creamily*) Your Majesty, Count Rosenberg is very worried that if this music is put back it will create the most unfortunate precedent. One will have thereafter to endure hours of dancing in opera.

Joseph I think we can guard against that, you know, Chamberlain. I really think we can guard against hours of dancing. (*To Orsini-Rosenberg*) Please restore Herr Mozart's music.

Orsini-Rosenberg But Majesty, I must insist——

Joseph (*with a touch of anger*) You will oblige me, Rosenberg! I wish to hear Mozart's music. Do you understand me?

Orsini-Rosenberg Yes, Majesty.

Mozart explodes with joy, jumps over a chair and throws himself at Joseph's feet

Mozart Oh God, I thank your Majesty! (*He kisses the Emperor's hand extravagantly, as at their first meeting*) Oh thank you—thank you—thank you, Sire, forever!

Joseph (*withdrawing his hand*) Yes, yes—very good. A little less enthusiasm, I beg you!

Mozart (*abashed*) Excuse me.

The Emperor rises. All follow suit

Joseph Well. *There it is!*

* * * *

The First Performance of Figaro

The Theatre glows with light for the first performance of Figaro

Servants enter and arrange the golden chairs in rows behind three chairs C. *Two chairs are placed* R *side by side, apart from the rest, to form Salieri's box*

Citizens come in swiftly together with Kapellmeister Bonno, Katherina Cavalieri, the Venticelli, Constanze and Teresa

The Emperor and his court quickly resume their seats and the others quickly take theirs. In the front row we note Katherina, all plumes and sequins, and

Bonno, older than ever. Behind them sit Constanze and the Venticelli. Salieri's good wife Teresa—more statuesque than ever—sits on the chair UR. *All of them stare out at the Audience as if it were the opera they have come to see: the people of fashion down the front and the poorer people crowded into the Light Box*

Salieri (*crossing to his box, to the Audience*) And so *Figaro* was produced in spite of all my efforts. I sat in my box and watched it happen. A conspicuous defeat for me. And yet I was strangely excited.

Faintly we hear Figaro singing the tune of "Non piu andrai". The stage audience is obviously delighted: they smile out front as they watch the (invisible) action

My march! My poor "March of Welcome"—now set to enchant the world forever!

It fades. Applause. The Emperor rises, and with him the stage audience, to denote an intermission. Joseph greets Katherina and Bonno. Orsini-Rosenberg and von Strack go to Salieri's box

Orsini-Rosenberg (*to Salieri*) Almost in your style, that last bit. But more vulgar of course. Far more obvious than you would ever be.
Von Strack (*drawling*) Exactly!

A bell rings for the end of the intermission. The Emperor returns quickly to his seat. The stage audience sits. A pause. All look out front, unmoving

Salieri (*raptly and quietly; to the Audience*) Trembling, I heard the second act. (*Pause*) The restored third act. (*Pause*) The astounding fourth. What shall I say to you who will one day hear this last act for yourselves? You will—because whatever else shall pass away, this must remain.

Faintly we hear the solemn closing ensemble from Act Four of Figaro, *"Ah! Tutti contenti. Saremo cosi"*

(*Over this*) The scene was night in a summer garden. Pinprick stars gleamed down on shaking summerhouses. Plotters glided behind pasteboard hedges. I saw a woman, dressed in her maid's clothes, hear her husband utter the first tender words he has offered her in years only because he thinks she is someone else. Could one catch a realer moment? And how except in a net of pure artifice? The disguises of opera had been invented for Mozart. (*He can barely look out at the "stage"*) The final reconciliation melted sight. (*Pause*) Through my tears I saw the Emperor— yawn.

Joseph yawns. The music fades. There is scant applause. Joseph rises and the courtiers follow suit. Mozart bows

Joseph (*coolly*) Most ingenious, Mozart. You are coming along nicely ... I do think we must omit encores in future. It really makes things far too long. Make a note, Rosenberg.
Orsini-Rosenberg Majesty.

Mozart lowers his head, crushed

Joseph Gentlemen, good-night to you. Strack, attend me.

> *Joseph goes out with von Strack. Director Orsini-Rosenberg gives Mozart one triumphant look and follows*

Salieri nods to his wife

> *Teresa leaves with the rest of the stage audience. Only Constanze lingers for a second, then she too goes*

A pause. Mozart and Salieri are left alone: Salieri deeply shaken by the opera, Mozart deeply upset by its reception. He crosses and sits next to Salieri

Mozart (*low*) Herr Salieri.
Salieri Yes?
Mozart What do you think? Do you think I am coming along nicely?
Salieri (*moved*) I think the piece is ... extraordinary. I think it is ... *marvellous.* Yes.

Pause. Mozart turns to him

Mozart I'll tell you what it is. It's the best opera yet written. That's what it is. And only I could have done it. No-one else living!

Salieri turns his head swiftly, as if he has been slapped. Mozart rises and walks away. The Lights change

> *The Venticelli rush on*

Salieri and Mozart both freeze

Venticello 1 Rosenberg is furious.
Venticello 2 He'll never forgive Mozart.
Venticello 1 He'll do anything to get back at him!
Salieri (*rising; to the Audience*) So it wasn't hard to get the piece cancelled. I saw to it through the person of the resentful Director that in the entire year *Figaro* was played only *nine times*! ... My defeat finally turned into a victory. And God's response to my challenge remained as inscrutable as ever ... Was He taking any notice of me at *all*? ...

Mozart breaks his freeze and comes downstage

> *Servants come on and clear the golden chairs off stage*

Mozart *Withdrawn!* Absolutely no plans for its revival!
Salieri I commiserate with you, my friend. But if the public does not like one's work, one has to accept the fact gracefully. (*Aside, to the Audience*) And certainly they didn't.
Venticello 1 (*complaining*) It's too complicated!
Venticello 2 (*complaining*) Too tiresome!
Venticello 1 All those weird harmonies!
Venticello 2 And never a good bang at the end of songs so you know when to clap!

The Venticelli go off

Salieri (*to the Audience*) Obviously I would not need to plot too hard against his operas in future. The Viennese could be relied upon to destroy those for me. I must concentrate on the man. I decided to see him as much as possible; to learn everything I could of his weaknesses.

*   *   *   *

The Waldstädten Library

Servants again bring on the wing-chair, place it as before and exit

Mozart I'll go to England. England loves music. That's the answer!

Salieri (*to the Audience*) We were yet again in the library of the Baroness Waldstädten: that room fated to be the scene of ghastly encounters between us. Again, took the compensating *crema al mascarpone*. (*He sits in the chair and eats greedily*)

Mozart I was there when I was a boy. They absolutely adored me. I had more kisses than you've had cakes! . . . When I was a child, people loved me.

Salieri Perhaps they will again. Why don't you go to London and try?

Mozart Because I have a wife and child and no money. I wrote to Papa to take the boy off my hands just for a few months so I could go—and he refused! . . . In the end everyone betrays you. Even the man you think loves you best . . . He's a bitter man, of course. After he'd finished showing me off around Europe he never went anywhere himself. He just stayed up in Salzburg year after year, kissing the ring of the fartsbishop and lecturing me! . . . (*Confidentially*) The real thing is, you see, he's jealous. Under everything he's jealous of me! He'll never forgive me for being cleverer than he is. (*He leans excitedly over Salieri's chair like a naughty child*) I'll tell you a secret. Leopold Mozart is just a jealous, dried up old turd . . . And I actually detest him. (*He giggles guiltily*)

The Venticelli appear quickly

They address Salieri as Mozart freezes

Venticello 1 (*solemnly*) Leopold Mozart——
Venticello 2 (*solemnly*) Leopold Mozart——
Venticello 1 ⎞
                 ⎟ (*together*)⎰*Leopold Mozart is dead!*
Venticello 2 ⎠

The Venticelli go off

Mozart recoils. A long pause

Salieri Do not despair. Death is inevitable, my friend.

Mozart (*desperately*) How will I go now?

Salieri What do you mean?

Mozart In the world. There's no-one else. No-one who understands the wickedness around. *I can't see it!* . . . He watched for me all my life—and I betrayed him.

Salieri No!
Mozart I talked against him.
Salieri No!
Mozart (*distressed*) I married where he begged me not. I left him alone. I danced and played billiards and fooled about, and he sat by himself night after night in an empty house, and no woman to care for him . . .

Salieri rises in concern and puts the bowl down on the little table

Salieri Wolfgang. My dear Wolfgang. Don't accuse yourself! . . . Lean upon me, if you care to . . . Lean upon me.

Salieri opens his arms in a wide gesture of paternal benevolence. Mozart approaches, and is almost tempted to surrender to the embrace. But at the last moment he avoids it, and breaks away down front, to fall on his knees

Mozart *Papa!*
Salieri (*to the Audience*) So rose the Ghost Father in *Don Giovanni!*

*   *   *   *

The two grim chords which open the overture to Don Giovanni *sound through the theatre. Mozart seems to quail under them, as he stares out front and sinks to his knees. On the backdrop in the Light Box appears the silhouette of a giant black figure, in cloak and tricorne hat. It extends its arms, menacingly and engulfingly, towards its begetter*

Salieri A father more accusing than any in opera. So rose the figure of a Guilty Libertine, cast into Hell! . . . I looked on astounded as from his ordinary life he made his art. We were both ordinary men, he and I. Yet he from the ordinary created legends—and I from legends created only the ordinary.

The figure fades. Salieri stands over the kneeling Mozart

Could I not have stopped my war? Shown him some pity? Oh yes, my friends, at any time—if He above had shown me one drop of it! Every day I set to work I prayed—I still prayed, you understand—"Make this one good in my ears! Just this one! *One!*" But would He ever? . . . I heard my music calmed in convention—not one breath of spirit to lift it off the shallows. And I heard *his*—

We hear the exquisite strains of the Terzetto "Soave il Vento" from Cosi Fan Tutte

The spirit singing through it unstoppable to my ears alone! I heard his comedy of the seduction of two sisters, *Cosi Fan Tutte: Thus do all* women. Aloysia and Constanze immortalized—two average girls turned into divinities: their sounds of surrender sweeter than the psalms of Heaven. (*To God, in anguish*) "Grant this to me! . . . *Grant this to me!* . . ." (*As "God"*) "No, no, no: I do not need you, Salieri! I have Mozart! Better for you to be silent!" *Hahahahaha!*

The music cuts off

The Creature's dreadful giggle was the laughter of God. I had to end it. But how? There was only one way. *Starvation.* Reduce the man to destitution. Starve out the God!

Servants enter and remove the wing-chair

*   *   *   *

Vienna and the Palace of Schönbrunn

Unseen, the Emperor enters the Light Box and takes up his position

Salieri (*to Mozart*) How do you fare today?
Mozart Badly. I have no money, and no prospect of any.
Salieri It would not be too hard, surely.

The Lights come up on the Palace of Schönbrunn. The Emperor stands in the Light Box, in his golden space

Joseph We must find him a post.
Salieri (*to the Audience*) One danger! The Emperor.

Salieri goes upstage to Joseph

There's nothing available, Majesty.
Joseph There's Chamber Composer now that Gluck is dead.
Salieri (*shocked*) Mozart to follow Gluck?
Joseph I won't have him say I drove him away. You know what a tongue he has.
Salieri Then grant him Gluck's post, Majesty, but not his salary. That would be wrong.
Joseph Gluck got two thousand florins a year. What should Mozart get?
Salieri Two hundred. Light payment, yes, but for light duties.
Joseph Perfectly fair. I'm obliged to you, Court Composer.
Salieri (*bowing*) Majesty.

The Lights go down a little on Joseph who still stands there. Salieri returns to Mozart

(*To the Audience*) Easily done. Like many men obsessed with being thought generous, the Emperor Joseph was quintessentially stingy.

Mozart goes and kneels before the Emperor

Joseph Herr Mozart. *Vous nous faîtes honneur!* . . .

The Lights go down on the Emperor. Mozart turns and walks downstage

Mozart It's a damned insult! Not enough to keep a mouse in cheese for a week!
Salieri Regard it as a token, *caro* Herr.
Mozart When I was young they gave me snuff boxes. Now it's tokens! And for what? Pom-pom, for fireworks! Twang-twang for contredanzes!
Salieri I'm sorry it's made you angry. I'd not have suggested it if I'd known you'd be distressed.

Mozart You suggested it?

Salieri I regret I was not able to do more.

Mozart Oh ... forgive me! You're a good man! I see that now! You're a truly kind man—and I'm a monstrous fool! (*He grasps Salieri's hand*)

Salieri No, please ...

Mozart You make me ashamed ... You excellent man!

Salieri (*imitating the Emperor*) No, no, no, no—*s'il vous plaît*. A little less enthusiasm I beg you!

Mozart laughs delightedly at this. Salieri joins in. Mozart suddenly doubles over with stomach cramps. He groans

   Wolfgang! What is it?

Mozart I get cramps sometimes in my stomach.

Salieri I'm sorry.

Mozart Excuse me ... it's nothing really.

Salieri I will see you soon again?

Mozart Of course.

Salieri Why not visit me?

Mozart I will ... I promise!

Salieri *Bene.*

Mozart *Bene.*

Salieri My friend. My new friend.

   Mozart giggles with pleasure and goes off

A pause

Salieri (*to the Audience*) Now if ever was the moment for God to crush me. I waited—and do you know what happened? I had just ruined Mozart's career at court; God rewarded me by granting my dearest wish!

   The Venticelli come on

   Von Strack and Orsini-Rosenberg enter the Light Box unseen and take up their positions.

Venticello 1 Kapellmeister Bonno.

Venticello 2 Kapellmeister Bonno.

Venticello 1 }
Venticello 2 } (*together*) {*Kapellmeister Bonno is dead!*

Salieri opens his mouth in surprise

Venticello 1 You are appointed—

Venticello 2 By Royal Decree—

Venticello 1 To fill his place.

The Lights come up full on the Emperor in the Light Box. He is flanked by von Strack and Orsini-Rosenberg standing like icons as at their first appearance

Salieri turns and bows to the Emperor

Joseph (*formally to Salieri*) First Royal and Imperial Kapellmeister to our court.

The Venticelli applaud

Venticello 1 Bravo.
Venticello 2 Bravo.
Orsini-Rosenberg *Evviva, Salieri!*
Von Strack Well done, Salieri!
Joseph (*warmly*) Dear Salieri—there it is!

The Lights go down on the Palace of Schönbrunn

> *In the dark, the Emperor, von Strack and Orsini-Rosenberg exit for the last time*

Salieri turns round, alarmed

Salieri (*to the Audience*) I was now truly alarmed. How long would I go unpunished?
Venticello 1 ⎫ (*together*) ⎧ Congratulations, sir!
Venticello 2 ⎭   ⎩
Venticello 1 Mozart looks appalling.
Venticello 2 It must be galling of course.
Venticello 1 I hear he's dosing himself constantly with medicine.
Salieri For what?
Venticello 2 Envy, I imagine.
Venticello 1 I hear there's another child on the way . . .
Venticello 2 There is, I've seen the mother.

*   *   *   *

The Prater

Fresh green trees appear on the backdrop. The Lights change to yellow, turning the blue surround into a rich verdant green

> *Mozart and Constanze enter arm-in-arm. She is palpably pregnant and wears a poor coat and bonnet; his clothes are poorer too. Salieri promenades with the Venticelli*

Salieri I met him next in the Prater.
Mozart (*to Salieri*) Congratulations, sir!
Salieri I thank you. And to you both! (*To the Audience*) Clearly there was a change for the worse. His eyes gleamed, oddly, like a dog's when the light catches. (*To Mozart*) I hear you are not well, my friend.

He acknowledges Constanze, who curtsies to him

Mozart I'm not. My pains stay with me.
Salieri How wretched. What can they be?
Mozart Also, I sleep badly . . . I have . . . bad dreams.
Constanze (*warningly*) Wolferl!
Salieri Dreams?
Mozart Always the same one . . . A figure comes to me cloaked in grey—doing this. (*He beckons slowly*) It has no face. Just grey—like, a mask . . . (*He giggles nervously*) What can it mean, do you think?

Salieri Surely you do not believe in dreams?

Mozart No, of course not—really!

Salieri Surely *you* do not, madame?

Constanze I never dream, sir. Things are unpleasant enough to me, awake.

Salieri bows

Mozart It's all fancy, of course!

Constanze If Wolfgang had proper work he might dream less, First Kapellmeister.

Mozart (*embarrassed, taking her arm*) Stanzi, please! ... Excuse us, sir. Come, dearest. We are well enough, thank you!

Husband and wife go off

Venticello 1 He's growing freakish.

Venticello 2 No question.

Venticello 1 Grey figures with masked faces!

Salieri (*looking after Mozart*) He broods on his father too much, I fancy. Also his circumstances make him anxious.

Venticello 1 They've moved house again.

Venticello 2 To the Rauhensteingasse. Number nine-seventy.

Venticello 1 They must be desperate.

Venticello 2 It's a real slum.

Salieri Does he earn any money at all, apart from his Post?

Venticello 1 Nothing whatever.

Venticello 2 I hear he's starting to beg.

Venticello 1 They say he's written letters to twenty Brother Masons.

Salieri Really?

Venticello 2 And they're giving him money.

Salieri (*to the Audience*) Of course! They *would*! ... I had *forgotten* the Masons! *Naturally* they would relieve him—*how stupid of me*! ... There could be no finally starving him with the Masons there to help! As long as he asked they would keep supplying his wants! ... How could I stop it? And quickly! ...

Venticello 1 Lord Fugue is most displeased with him!

Salieri *Is* he?

*   *   *   *

A Masonic Lodge

A Servant brings on a Masonic apron which he gives to Salieri who puts it on

A huge golden emblem encrusted with Masonic symbols descends

Van Swieten enters. He is wearing the ritual apron over his sober clothes. At the same time Mozart enters R. He too wears the apron. The two men clasp hands in fraternal greeting

Van Swieten (*gravely*) This is not good, Brother. The lodge was not created for you to beg from.

Mozart What else can I do?

Van Swieten Give concerts, as you used to do.

Mozart I have no subscribers left, Baron. I am no longer fashionable.

Van Swieten I am not surprised. You write tasteless comedies which give offence. I warned you, often enough.

Mozart (*humbly*) You did. I admit it. (*He holds his stomach in pain*)

Van Swieten I will send you some fugues of Bach tomorrow. You can arrange those for my Sunday concert. You shall have a small fee.

Mozart Thank you, Baron.

Van Swieten nods and goes out

Salieri steps forward

(*Shouting after van Swieten*) I cannot live by arranging Bach!

Salieri (*sarcastically*) A generous fellow.

Mozart All the same, I'll have to do it. If he were to turn the lodge against me, I'd be finished. My Brother Masons virtually keep me now.

Salieri That's fine.

Mozart Never mind. I'll manage: you'll see! Things are looking up already. I've had a marvellous proposal from Schickaneder. He's a new member of this lodge.

Salieri Schickaneder? The actor?

Mozart Yes. He owns a theatre in the suburbs.

Salieri Well, more of a music hall, surely?

Mozart Yes ... He wants me to write him a vaudeville—something for ordinary German people. Isn't that a wonderful idea? ... He's offered me half the receipts when we open.

Salieri Nothing in advance?

Mozart He said he couldn't afford anything. I know it's not much of an offer. But a popular piece about brotherly love could celebrate everything we believe as Masons!

Salieri It certainly could! ... Why don't you put the Masons *into* it?

Mozart Into an opera? ... I couldn't!

Salieri laughs, to indicate that he was simply making a joke

All the same—what an idea!

Salieri (*earnestly*) Our rituals are secret, Wolfgang.

Mozart I needn't copy them exactly. I could adapt them a little.

Salieri Well ... It would certainly be in a great cause.

Mozart Brotherly love!

Salieri Brotherly love!

They both turn and look solemnly at the great golden emblem hanging at their backs

(*Warmly*) Try it and see. Take courage, Wolfgang. It's a glorious idea.

Mozart It is, isn't it? It *really is*!

Salieri Of course say nothing till it's done.

Mozart Not a word.

Salieri (*making a sign: a closed fist*) Secret!
Mozart (*making a similar sign*) Secret!
Salieri Good. (*He steps out of the scene downstage. To the Audience*) And if
that didn't finish him off with the Masons—nothing would!

The golden emblem withdraws. We hear the merry dance of Monastatos from
The Magic Flute: *"Das Klinget so herrlich, Das Klinget so schön!"*

*To the tinkling of the glockenspiel Servants bring on a long plain table
loaded with manuscripts and bottles. It also bears a plain upturned stool, a
chair with cushions and a blanket. They place this in the wooden area head-
on to the Audience and then take away Mozart's Masonic apron*

*At the same time Constanze appears wearily upstage, and enters this
apartment: the Rauhensteingasse. She wears a stuffed apron, indicating the
advanced state of her pregnancy*

*Simultaneously, two other Servants bring on three gilded chairs which they
place upstage R and then set the small gilded table with the loaded cake-
stand next to them. We now have in view the two contrasting apartments. A
Servant takes away Salieri's apron*

As soon as the emblem withdraws the Venticelli appear to Salieri

* * * *

Mozart's Apartment; Salieri's Apartments

Venticello 1 Mozart is delighted with himself!
Venticello 2 He's writing a secret opera!
Venticello 1 (*crossly*) And won't tell anyone its theme.
Venticello 2 It's really too tiresome.

The Venticelli go off

Salieri He told me. He told me everything! ... Initiation ceremonies.
Ceremonies with blindfolds. All rituals copied from the Masons! ... He
sat at home preparing his own destruction. A home where life grew daily
more grim.

*He goes upstage and sits on one of his gilded chairs, devouring a cake. Mozart
also sits at his table, wrapped in a blanket, and starts to write music. Opposite
him Constance sits on a stool, wrapped in a shawl*

Constanze I'm cold ... I'm cold all day ... hardly surprising since we have
no firewood.
Mozart Papa was right. We end exactly as he said. Beggars.
Constanze It's all his fault.
Mozart Papa's?
Constanze He kept you a baby all your life.
Mozart I don't understand. You always loved Papa.
Constanze Did I?
Mozart You adored him. You told me so often.

Slight pause

Constanze (*flatly*) I hated him.
Mozart What?
Constanze And he hated me.
Mozart That's absurd. He loved us both very much. You're being extremely silly now.
Constanze Am I?
Mozart (*airily*) Yes, you are, little-wife-of-my-heart!
Constanze Do you remember the fire we had last night, because it was so cold you couldn't even get the ink wet? You said, "What a blaze"—remember? "What a blaze! All those old papers going up!" Well, my dear, those old papers were just all your father's letters, that's all—every one he wrote since the day we married.
Mozart *What?*
Constanze Every one! All the letters about what a ninny I am—what a bad housekeeper I am! Every one!
Mozart (*crying out*) Stanzi!
Constanze *Shit on him! ... Shit on him!*
Mozart *You bitch!*
Constanze (*savagely*) At least it kept us warm! What else will do that? Perhaps we should dance! You love to dance, Wolferl—let's dance! Dance to keep warm! (*Grandly*) Write me a contredanze, Mozart! It's your job to write dances, isn't it? (*Hysterical, she starts dancing roughly round the room like a demented peasant to the tune of "Non più andrai". She sings wildly*) "Non più andrai, farfallone amoroso—Notte e giorno d'intorno girando!"
Mozart (*shrieking*) Stop it! Stop it! (*He seizes her*) Stanzi-marini! Marini-bini! Don't, please. Please, please, please I beg you ... Look there's a kiss! Where's it coming from? Right out of that corner! There's another one—all wet, all sloppy wet coming straight to *you*! Kiss—kiss—kiss!

She pushes him away. Constanze dances. Mozart catches her

Constanze (*pushing him away*) Get off!

Pause

Mozart I'm frightened, Stanzi. Something awful's happening to me.
Constanze I can't bear it. I can't bear much more of this.
Mozart And the figure's like this now—(*beckoning faster*)—"Here! Come here! Here!" Its face still masked—invisible! It becomes realer and realer to me!
Constanze Stop it, for God's sake! ... Stop! ... It's me who's frightened ... *Me!* ... You frighten me ... If you go on like this I'll leave you. I swear it.
Mozart (*shocked*) Stanzi!
Constanze I mean it ... I do ... (*She puts her hand to her stomach, as if in pain*)
Mozart I'm sorry ... Oh God, I'm sorry ... I'm sorry, I'm sorry, I'm sorry! ... Come here to me, little-wife-of-my-heart! Come ... Come ...

He kneels and coaxes her to him. She comes half-reluctantly, half-willingly

Who am I? . . . Quick: tell me. Hold me and tell who I am.
Constanze Pussy-wussy.
Mozart Who else?
Constanze Miaowy-powy.
Mozart And you're squeeky-peeky. And Stanzi-manzi. And Bini-gini!

She surrenders

Constanze Wolfi-polfi!
Mozart Poopy–peepee!

They giggle

Constanze Now don't be stupid.
Mozart (*insistent: like a child*) Come on—do it. Do it . . . Let's do it. Poppy!

They play a private game, gradually doing it faster, on their knees

Constanze Poppy.
Mozart (*changing it*) Pappy.
Constanze (*copying*) Pappy.
Mozart Pappa.
Constanze Pappa.
Mozart Pappa-pappa!
Constanze Pappa-pappa!
Mozart Pappa-pappa-pappa-pappa!
Constanze Pappa-pappa-pappa-pappa!

They rub noses

Mozart } (*together*) { Pappa-pappa-pappa-pappa!
Constanze } { Pappa-pappa-pappa-pappa!
Constanze *Ah!* (*She suddenly cries out in distress, and clutches her stomach*)
Mozart Stanzi! . . . Stanzi, what is it?

The Venticelli hurry in

During the following, Constanze divests herself of her stuffed apron (thereby ceasing to be pregnant) and slowly rises

Venticello 1 News!
Venticello 2 Suddenly!
Venticello 1 She's been delivered.
Venticello 2 Unexpectedly.
Venticello 1 Of a boy!
Venticello 2 Poor little imp.
Venticello 1 To be born to that couple.
Venticello 2 In that room.
Venticello 1 With that money.
Venticello 2 And the father a baby himself.

Constanze turns sorrowfully and walks slowly upstage and goes out, taking the apron with her

Mozart follows her for a few steps, alarmed. He halts

Venticello 1 And now I hear—
Venticello 2 Now I hear—
Venticello 1 Something more has happened.
Venticello 2 Even stranger.

Mozart picks up a bottle, then moves swiftly into Salieri's room

Mozart (*wildly*) She's gone!
Salieri What do you mean?

The Venticelli go off

Mozart (*sitting on one of the gilded chairs*) Stanzerl's gone away! Just for a while, she says. She's taken the baby and gone to Baden. To the spa . . . It will cost us the last money we have!
Salieri But *why*?
Mozart She's right to go . . . It's my fault . . . She thinks I'm mad.
Salieri Surely not?
Mozart Perhaps I am . . . I think I am . . . Yes . . .
Salieri Wolfgang . . .
Mozart (*very disturbed*) Let me tell you! Last night I saw the figure again— the figure in my dreams. Only this time I was *awake*! It stood before my table, all in grey, its face still grey, still masked. And this time it spoke to me! "Wolfgang Mozart—you must write now a Requiem Mass. Take up your pen and begin!"
Salieri A Requiem?
Mozart I asked, "Who is this Requiem for, who has died?" It said, "The work must be finished, when you see me next!" Then it turned and left the room!
Salieri Oh, this is morbid fancy, my friend!
Mozart It had the force of real things! . . . To tell the truth—I do not know whether it happened in my head or out of it . . . No wonder Stanzi has gone. I frightened her away . . . And now she'll miss the vaudeville.
Salieri You mean it's finished? So soon?
Mozart Oh, yes—music is easy: it's marriage that's hard!
Salieri I long to see it!
Mozart Would you come, truly? The theatre isn't grand. It's just a popular music hall. No-one from court will be there.
Salieri Do you think that matters to me? I would travel anywhere for a work by you! . . . I am no substitute for your little wife—but I know someone who could be!

He gets up. Mozart rises also

Mozart Who?
Salieri I'll tell you what—I'll bring Katherina! She'll cheer you up!
Mozart Katherina!
Salieri As I remember it, you quite enjoyed her company!

Mozart laughs heartily

Katherina Cavalieri enters, now fatter and wearing an elaborate plumed hat

She curtsies to Mozart and takes his arm

Mozart (*bowing*) *Signora!*
Salieri (*to the Audience*) And so to the opera we went—a strange band of three!

The other two freeze

The First Kapellmeister—sleek as a cat. His mistress—now fat and feathered like a great songbird she'd become. And Mozart, demented and drunk on the cheap wine which was now his constant habit.

They unfreeze

We went out into the suburbs—to a crowded music hall—in a tenement ...

*　　*　　*　　*

The Theatre by the Weiden

Servants bring in two benches and place them downstage. There is sudden noise and a crowd of working-class Germans swarm in from upstage: a chattering mass of humanity through which the three have to push their way to the front. The long table is pushed horizontally, and the rowdy stage audience piles on top of it, smoking pipes and chewing sausages

Unobserved, van Swieten comes in and stands at the back

Mozart You must be indulgent now! It's my first piece of this kind!

The three sit on the front bench: Mozart sick and emaciated; Cavalieri blowsy and bedizened; Salieri as elegant as ever

Salieri We sat as he wished us to, among ordinary Germans! The smell of meat and sausage was almost annihilating!

Cavalieri presses a mouchoir *to her sensitive nose*

(*To Mozart*) This is so exciting!
Mozart (*happily*) Do you think so?
Salieri (*looking about him*) Oh yes! This is exactly the audience we should be writing for! Not the dreary court ... As always—*you* show the way!

The stage audience freezes

(*To us*) As always, he did. My pungent neighbours *rolled* on their benches at the jokes—

They unfreeze, briefly, to demonstrate this mirth

And I alone in their midst heard—*The Magic Flute.*

They freeze again. The great hymn at the end of Act 2 is heard: "Heil sei euch Geweihten."

He <u>had</u> put the Masons into it right enough. Oh, yes—but how? He had turned them into an Order of Eternal Priests. I heard voices calling out of ancient temples. I saw a vast sun rise on a timeless land, where animals danced and children floated: and by its rays all the poisons we feed each other drawn up and burnt away!

A great sun does indeed rise inside the Light Box, and standing in it the gigantic silhouette of a priestly figure extending its arms to the world in universal greeting

And in this sun—behold—I saw his father. No more an accusing figure, but forgiving! The Highest Priest of the Order—his hand extended to the world in love! Wolfgang feared Leopold no longer: a final legend had been made! ... Oh the sound—the sound of that newfound peace in him— mocking my undiminishing pain! *There* was the Magic Flute—*there beside me*! (*He points to Mozart*)

Applause from all. Mozart jumps up excitedly on to the bench and acknowledges the clapping with his arms flung out. He turns to us, a bottle in his hand—his eyes staring: all freeze again

Mozart the flute, and God the relentless player. How long could the Creature stand it—so frail, so palpably mortal? ... And what was this I was tasting suddenly? Could it be pity? ... *Never!*

Van Swieten (*calling out*) Mozart!

Van Swieten pushes his way to the front through the crowd of dispersing Citizens. He is outraged

Mozart (*turning joyfully to greet him*) Baron! You here! How wonderful of you to come!

Van Swieten (*with cold fury*) What have you done?

Mozart Excellency?

Van Swieten You have put our rituals into a vulgar show!

Mozart No, sir—

Van Swieten They are plain for all to see! And to laugh at! You have betrayed the Order.

Mozart (*in horror*) NO!

Salieri Baron, a word with you—

Van Swieten Don't speak for him, Salieri! (*To Mozart, with frozen contempt*) You were ever a cruel vulgarian we hoped to mend. Stupid, hopeless task! Now you are a betrayer as well. I shall never forgive you. And depend upon it—I shall ensure that no Freemason or person of distinction will do so in Vienna so long as I have life!

Salieri Baron, please, I must speak!

Van Swieten No, sir! Leave alone. (*To Mozart*) I did not look for this reward, Mozart. Never speak to me.

Van Swieten goes out. The crowd disperses and goes off

The Lights change

Servants come on and remove the benches and stool

Salieri, watching Mozart narrowly, dismisses Katherina. Mozart stands as one dead

Katherina exits

Salieri Wolfgang? . . .

Mozart shakes his head sharply and walks away from him, upstage, desolate and stunned

Wolfgang—all is not lost.

Mozart enters his apartment and freezes

(*To the Audience*) But of course it was! Now he was ruined. Broken and shunned by all men of influence. And for good measure, he did not even get his half receipts from the opera.

*   *   *   *

Mozart's Apartment

The Venticelli come in

Venticello 1 Schickaneder pays him nothing.
Venticello 2 Schickaneder cheats him.
Venticello 1 Gives him enough for liquor.
Venticello 2 And keeps all the rest.
Salieri I couldn't have managed it better myself.

Mozart takes up a blanket and muffles himself in it. Then he sits at his work-table, down front, staring out at the Audience, quiet still, the blanket almost over his face

And then silence. No word came from him at all. Why? . . . I waited each day. Nothing. Why? . . . (*To the Venticelli, brusquely*) What does he do?

Mozart writes

Venticello 1 He sits at his window.
Venticello 2 All day and all night.
Venticello 1 Writing—
Venticello 2 Writing—like a man possessed.

Mozart springs to his feet, and freezes

Venticello 1 Springs up every moment!
Venticello 2 Stares wildly at the street!
Venticello 1 Expecting something—
Venticello 2 Someone—
Venticello 1 } (*together*) { We can't imagine what!
Venticello 2 }
Salieri (*to the Audience*) I could! (*He also springs up excitedly, dismissing the Venticelli*)

The Venticelli exit

Mozart and Salieri now both stand staring out front

Who did he look for? A figure in grey, masked and sorrowing, come to take him away. I knew what he was doing, alone in that slum! He was writing his Requiem Mass—for *himself*! . . . (*After a pause*) And now I confess the wickedest thing I did to him.

His Valet brings him the clothes which he describes, and he puts them on, turning his back to us to don the hat—to which is attached a mask. The Valet goes off

My friends—there is no blasphemy a man will not commit, compelled to such a war as mine! . . . I got me a cloak of grey . . . Yes. I got me a hat of grey. Yes. And a mask of grey—Yes!

He turns round: he is masked

And appeared myself to the demented Creature as—the *Messenger of God*! . . . I confess that in November, seventeen ninety-one, I—Antonio Salieri, then as now First Royal Kapellmeister to the Empire—walked empty Vienna in the freezing moonlight for seven nights on end! That precisely as the clocks of the city struck one I would halt beneath Mozart's window—and become his more terrible clock.

The clock strikes one. Salieri, without moving from R, raises his arms: his fingers show seven days. Mozart rises—fascinated and appalled—and stands equally rigidly L, looking out in horror

Every night I showed him one day less—then stalked away. Every night the face he showed me at the glass was more crazed. Finally—with no days left to him—*horror*! I arrived as usual. Halted. And instead of fingers, reached up beseechingly as the future of his dreams! "Come!—Come!—Come! . . ." (*He beckons to Mozart, insidiously*) He stood swaying, as if he would faint off into death. But suddenly—incredibly—he realized all his little strength, and in a clear voice called down to me the words out of his opera *Don Giovanni*, inviting the statue to dinner.

Mozart (*pushing open the "window"*) O statua gentilissima—venite a cena! (*He beckons in his turn*)

Salieri For a long moment one terrified man looked at another. Then—unbelievably—I found myself nodding, just as in the opera. Starting to move across the street!

The rising and falling scale passage from the overture to Don Giovanni *sounds darkly, looped in sinister repetition. To this hollow music Salieri marches slowly upstage*

Pushing down the latch of his door—tramping up the stairs with stone feet. There was no stopping it. *I was in his dream!*

Mozart stands terrified by his table. Salieri throws open the "door". The Lights change instantly. Salieri stands still, staring impassively downstage. Mozart addresses him urgently, and in awe

Mozart It's not finished! . . . Not nearly! . . . Forgive me. Time was I could write a Mass in a week! . . . Give me one month more and it'll be done: I swear it! . . . He'll grant me that, surely? You can't want it unfinished! . . . Look—Look, see what I've done.

He snatches up the pages from the table and bring them eagerly to the Figure

Here's the Kyrie—that's finished! Take that to him—he'll see it's not unworthy! . . . Kyrie the first theme, Eleison the second. Both together make a double figure.

Unwillingly Salieri moves across the room—takes the pages, and sits behind the table in Mozart's chair, staring out front

Grant me time, I beg you! If you do, I swear I'll write a real piece of music. I know I've boasted I've written hundreds, but it's not true. I've written nothing finally good!

Salieri looks at the pages. Immediately we hear the sombre opening of the Requiem Mass. *Over this Mozart speaks*

Oh, it began so well, my life. Once the world was so full, so happy! . . . All the journeys—all the carriages—all the rooms of smiles! Everyone smiled at me once—the King at Schönbrunn; the Princess at Versailles—they lit my way with candles to the clavier!—my father bowing, bowing, bowing with such joy! . . . "Chevalier Mozart, my miraculous son!" . . . Why has it all gone? . . . Why? . . . Was I so bad? So wicked . . . (*Desperately*) Answer for him and tell me!

Deliberately Salieri tears the paper into halves. The music stops instantly. Silence

(*Fearfully*) Why? . . . Is it not good?
Salieri (*stiffly*) It is good. Yes. It is good.

He tears off a corner of the music paper, elevates it in the manner of the Communion Service, places it on his tongue and eats it

(*In pain*) I eat what God gives me. Dose after dose. For all of life. His poison. We are both poisoned, Amadeus. I with you: you with me.

In horror Mozart moves slowly behind him, placing his hand over Salieri's mouth—then, still from behind, slowly removes the mask and hat. Salieri stares at the Audience

Ecco mi. Antonio Salieri. Ten years of my hate have poisoned you to death.

Mozart falls to his knees, by the table

Mozart Oh God!
Salieri (*contemptuously*) God?! . . . God will not help you! God *does* not help!
Mozart Oh God! . . . Oh God! . . . Oh God!
Salieri God does not love you, Amadeus! God does not love! He can only

use! ... He cares nothing for who He uses: nothing for who He denies! ...
You are no use to Him anymore—You're too weak—too sick! He has
finished with you! All you can do now is *die!* He'll find another
instrument! He won't even remember you!

Mozart *Ah! (With a groan he crawls quickly through the trestle of the table,
like an animal finding a burrow—or a child a safe place of concealment)*

Salieri kneels by the table, calling in at his victim in desperation

Salieri Die, Amadeus! Die, I beg you, die! ... Leave me alone, *ti imploro!*
Leave me alone at last! Leave me alone! *(He beats on the table in his
despair)* Alone! Alone! Alone! Alone! Alone!

Mozart *(crying out at the top of his lungs)* PAPAAAAA! *(He freezes—his
mouth open in the act of screaming—his head staring out from under the
table)*

*Salieri rises in horror. Silence. Then very slowly, Mozart crawls out from
under the table. He sits. He sees Salieri. He smiles at him*

(In a childish voice) Papa!

Silence

Papa ... Papa ... *(He extends his arms upwards, imploringly to Salieri. He
speaks now as a very young boy)* Take me, Papa. Take me. Put down your
arms and I'll hop into them. Just as we used to do it! ... Hop-hop-hop-
hop-UP!

He jumps up on to the table, and embraces Salieri who stands in horror

Hold on close to you, Papa. Let's sing our little Kissing Song together.
Do you remember? ... *(He sings in an infantine voice) "Oragna figata fa!
Marina gamina fa!"*

Gently Salieri disengages himself

Salieri Reduce the man: reduce the God. Behold my vow fulfilled. The
profoundest voice in the world reduced to a nursery tune.

He leaves the room, slowly, as Mozart resumes his singing

Mozart *"Oragna figata fa! Marina gamina fa!"*

*Constanze enters upstage her bonnet in her hand and wearing a shawl. She
has returned from Baden. She comes downstage towards her husband, and
finds him there on the table, singing in an obviously childish treble*

*"Oragna figata fa! Marina gamina fa. Fa! Fa!" (He kisses the air, several
times. Finally he becomes aware of his wife standing beside him. Uncer-
tainly)* Stanzi?

Constanze Wolfi? ...

Mozart *(in relief)* Stanzi!

Constanze *(with great tenderness)* Wolfi—my love! Little husband of my
heart!

He virtually falls off the table into her arms

Mozart *Oh!*

He clings to her in overwhelming pleasure. She helps him gently to move around the table to the chair behind it, facing out front

Constanze Oh, my dear one—come with me ... Come on ... Come on now. There ... There ...

Mozart sits weakly

Mozart (*like a child still, and most earnestly*) Salieri ... Salieri has killed me.
Constanze Yes, my dear. (*Practically she busies herself clearing the table of its manuscripts, its candle, its bottles and its ink-well*)
Mozart He has. He told me so.
Constanze Yes, yes: I'm sure. (*She finds the chair cushions and places them at the right-hand head of the table*)
Mozart (*petulantly*) He did ... He did!
Constanze Hush now, lovely.

She helps her dying husband on to the table, now his bed. He lies down, and she covers him with her shawl

I'm back to take care of you. I'm sorry I went away. I'm here now, for always!
Mozart Salieri ... Salieri ... Salieri ... Salieri! (*He starts to weep*)
Constanze Oh lovey, be silent now. No-one has hurt you. You'll get better soon, I promise. Can you hear me? Try to, Wolferl ... Wolfi-polfi, please! ...

Faintly the Lacrimosa of the Requiem Mass *begins to sound. Mozart rises to hear it—leaning against his wife's shoulders. His hand begins feebly to beat out drum measures from the music. During the whole of the following it is evident that he is composing the Mass in his head, and does not hear his wife at all*

If I've been a bore—if I've nagged a bit about money, it didn't mean anything. It's only because I'm spoilt. You spoilt me, lovey. You've got to get well, Wolfi—because we need you. Karl and Baby Franz as well. There's only the three of us, lovey: we don't cost much. Just don't leave us—we wouldn't know what to do without you. And you wouldn't know much either, up in Heaven, without us. You soppy thing. You can't even cut up your own meat without help! ... I'm not clever, lovey. It can't have been easy living with a goose. But I've looked after you, you must admit that. And I've given you fun too—quite a lot really! ... Are you listening?

The drum strokes get slower, and stop

Know one thing. It was the best day of my life when you married me. And as long as I live I'll be the most honoured woman in the world ... Can you hear me?

She becomes aware that Mozart is dead. She opens her mouth in a silent scream, raising her arm in a rigid gesture of grief

The great chord of the "Amen" does not resolve itself, but lingers on in intense reverberation

*   *   *   *

The Citizens of Vienna come in L, *dressed in black*

Constanze kneels and freezes in grief as Servants come in and stand at the four corners of the table on which the body lies

Van Swieten also comes in

Salieri (*hard*) The Death Certificate said kidney failure, hastened by exposure to cold. Generous Lord Fugue paid for a pauper's funeral. Twenty other corpses. An unmarked limepit.

Van Swieten approaches Constanze

Van Swieten What little I can spare, you shall have for the children. There's no need to waste it on vain show.

The Servants lift the table and bear it, with its burden, upstage C, *to the Light Box. The Citizens follow it*

Salieri What did I feel? Relief, of course: I confess it. And pity too, for the man I helped to destroy. I felt the pity God can never feel. I weakened God's flute to thinness. God blew—as He must—without cease. The flute split in the mouth of His insatiable *need*!

The Citizens kneel. In dead silence the Servants throw Mozart's body off the table into the space at the back of the stage

Van Swieten and the Servants, taking the table with them go off

Constanze unfreezes and starts assiduously collecting the manuscripts and other items scattered all over the floor

Salieri now speaks with an increasingly ageing voice: a voice poisoned more and more by its own bitterness

As for Constanze, in the fullness of time she married again—a Danish diplomat as dull as a clock—and retired to Salzburg, birthplace of the Great Composer, to become the final authority in all matters Mozartian!

Constanze rises, wrapping her shawl about her, and clasping manuscripts to her bosom

Constanze (*reverentially*) A sweeter-tongued man never lived! In ten years of blissful marriage I never heard him utter a single coarse or conceited word. The purity of his life is reflected absolutely in the purity of his music! . . . (*More briskly*) In selling his manuscripts I charge by the ink. So many notes, so many schillings. That seem to me the simplest way.

She leaves the stage, a pillar of rectitude

Salieri One amazing fact emerged. Mozart did not *imagine* that masked figure in grey who said, "Take up your pen and write a Requiem". It was *real*! . . . A certain bizarre nobleman called Count Walsegg had a longing to be thought a composer. He actually sent his steward in disguise to Mozart to commission the piece—secretly, so that he could pass it off as his own work. And this he even did! After Mozart's death it was actually performed as Count Walsegg's Requiem . . . And I conducted it. (*He smiles at the Audience*) Naturally I did. In those days I presided over all great musical occasions in Vienna. (*He divests himself of his cloak*) I even conducted the salvoes of cannon in Beethoven's dreadful *Battle Symphony*. An experience which made me almost as deaf as he was!

The Citizens turn round and bow to him, kissing their hands extravagantly. During the following, they fall on their knees to him and all clap their hands at him silently in an adoring mime, relentlessly extending their arms upwards and upwards until they seem almost to obliterate him

And so I stayed on in the City of Musicians, reverenced by all! *On* and *on* and *on*! . . . *For thirty-two years!* . . . And slowly I understood the nature of God's punishment. (*Directly; to the Audience*) What had I asked for in that Church as a boy? Was it not fame? Well now I had it! I was to become quite simply the most famous musician in Europe! . . . I was to be bricked up in fame! Buried in fame! . . . Embalmed in fame—but for work I knew to be absolutely worthless! . . . This was my sentence! I must endure thirty years of being called "distinguished" by people incapable of distinguishing! . . . I must smell as I wrote it the deadness of my music, whilst their eyes brimmed with tears and their throats brayed with cheering! . . . And finally—when my nose had been rubbed in fame to vomiting—receptions, awards, civic medals and chains—: Suddenly His masterstroke!—*Silence!*

The Citizens freeze

It would all be taken away from me—every scrap.

The Citizens rise, turn away from him, and walk indifferently off

Mozart's music would sound everywhere—and mine in no place on earth. I must survive to see myself become *extinct*! . . . When they trundled me out in a carriage to get my last honour a man on the kerb said "Isn't that one of the generals from Waterloo?" (*Calling up savagely*) Nemico dei Nemici! Dio implacabile!

The curtains of the Light Box close

A Servant brings on the wheelchair and places it C *as before. Another Servant brings on Salieri's old dressing-robe shawl and cap*

Salieri divests himself of his wig and cloak and puts on the dressing-robe, shawl and cap, once more becoming the old man. He sits in the wheelchair

The Lights change. Six o'clock strikes

*   *   *   *

Salieri's Apartments

November 1823. Six o'clock

The Servants leave taking the wig and grey cloak and hat

Salieri Dawn has come. I must release you. One moment's violence and it is over. You see, I cannot accept this. To be sucked into oblivion—not even my name remembered. Oh no. I did not live on earth to be His joke for eternity. I have one trick left me:—see how He deals with this! (*Confidentially, to the Audience*) All this week I have been shouting out about murder. You heard me yourselves—do you remember? "Mozart—pietà! Pardon your assassin! Mozart!"

Whispers of "Salieri" begin: at first faintly, as at the start of the play. During the following they grow in volume, in strict and operatic counterpoint to Salieri's speeches

Whisperers (*faintly*) Salieri!
Salieri (*triumphantly*) I did this deliberately! . . . My servants carried the news into the streets!
Whisperers (*louder*) Salieri!
Salieri The streets repeated it to one another!
Whisperers (*louder*) Salieri! . . . Salieri!
Salieri Now my name is on every tongue! Vienna, City of Scandals, has a scandal worthy of it at last!
Whisperers SALIERI! . . . ASSASSIN! . . . ASSASSIN! . . . SALIERI!
Salieri (*falsetto; enjoying it*) "Can it be true? . . . Is it possible? . . . Did he do it after all? . . ."
Whisperers (*fortissimo*) SALIERI!!!
Salieri Well my friends, now they all will know for sure! They will learn of my dreadful death—and they will believe the lie forever! After today, whenever men speak Mozart's name with love, they will speak mine with loathing! As his name grows in the world so will mine—if not in fame, then in infamy. *I'm going to be immortal after all!*—And He is powerless to prevent it! . . . (*He laughs harshly*) So, *Signore*—see now if man is mocked!

He produces a razor from his pocket. Then he rises, opens it, and addresses the Audience most simply, gently, and directly

Amici cari. I was born a pair of ears, and nothing else. It is only through hearing music that I know God exists. Only through writing music that I could worship. . . . All around me men hunger for General Rights. I hungered only for particular notes. They seek Liberty for Mankind. I sought only slavery for myself. To be owned—ordered—exhausted by an Absolute. This was denied me—and with it all meaning. Now I go to become a ghost myself. I will stand in the shadows when you come here to this earth in your turns. And when you feel the dreadful bite of your failures—and hear the taunting of unachievable, uncaring God—I will whisper my name to you: "Antonio Salieri: Patron Saint of Mediocrities!" And in the depth of your downcastness you can pray to me. And I will forgive you. *Vi Saluto.* (*He cuts his throat and falls backwards into the wheelchair*)

The following three things happen almost simultaneously:

The Cook enters carrying a plate of buns for breakfast and seeing Salieri screams in horror

Mozart's sombre Masonic Funeral Music *plays faintly throughout the following*

The Valet rushes in from the opposite side

Together they pull the wheelchair, with its slumped body, backwards upstage, and anchor it C

The Venticelli appear again, in the costume of 1823. Venticello 1 carries books and a newspaper

Venticello 1 Beethoven's Conversation Book November eighteen twenty-three. Visitors write the news for the deaf man.

He hands a book to Venticello 2

Venticello 2 (*reading*) "Salieri has cut his throat—but is still alive!"

Salieri stirs and comes to life, looking about him bewilderedly

The Valet and Cook depart

Salieri stares out front like an astounded gargoyle

Venticello 1 Beethoven's Conversation Book, eighteen twenty-four. Visitors write the news for the deaf man.

He hands another book to Venticello 2

Venticello 2 (*reading*) "Salieri is quite deranged. He keeps claiming that he is guilty of Mozart's death, and made away with him by poison."

The Lights narrow to a bright cone, beating on Salieri

Venticello 1 The *German Musical Times*, May twenty-fifth, eighteen twenty-five.

He hands a newspaper to Venticello 2

Venticello 2 (*reading*) "Our worthy Salieri just cannot die. In the frenzy of his imagination he is even said to accuse himself of complicity in Mozart's early death. A rambling of the mind believed in truth by no-one but the deluded old man himself."

The music stops

Salieri lowers his head, conceding defeat

Venticello 1 I don't believe it.

Venticello 2 I don't believe it.
Venticello 1 I don't believe it.
Venticello 2 I don't believe it.
Venticello 1 ⎫ (*together*) ⎧ *No-one believes it in the world!*
Venticello 2 ⎭   ⎩

The Venticelli go off

The Lights dim a little. Salieri stirs, rises, comes down front and looks out far into the darkness of the theatre

Salieri Mediocrities everywhere—now and to come—I absolve you all. Amen! (*He extends his arms upwards and outwards to embrace the assembled Audience in a wide gesture of benediction—finally folding his arms high across his own breast*)

The Lights fade to Black-out and the last four chords of the Masonic Funeral Music *of Amadeus Mozart sound throughout the theatre*

CURTAIN

FURNITURE AND PROPERTY LIST

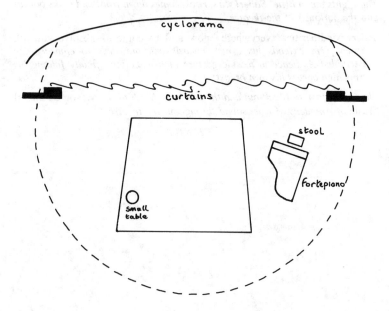

ACT I

VIENNA

On stage: Curtains of the Light Box open to start

Large chandelier suspended above the stage

Fortepiano with stool. *On fortepiano:* manuscript of **Salieri**'s "March of Welcome", old-fashioned round wooden ruler

On Wooden Rectangle

Small round gilded table DL. *On it:* filled cake-stand, small bowl of cream cheese with spoon

Eighteenth-century wheelchair UC

Personal: **Salieri:** 2 coins, *mouchoir* in court coat pocket

TRANSFORMATION TO THE EIGHTEENTH CENTURY

On stage: *In Light Box*

Golden chair C

Rolled paper (for **Joseph**)

Off stage: Wig-stand with powdered wig **(Servant)**
Upright chair **(Servant)**

THE PALACE OF SCHÖNBRUNN

Strike: *From Light Box*
Golden chair

THE LIBRARY OF THE BARONESS WALDSTÄDTEN

Off stage: Large table. *On it:* cakes, desserts **(Servants)**
High-backed wing-chair **(Servants)**

SALIERI'S APARTMENTS

Off stage: Manuscripts **(Venticelli)**

THE PALACE OF SCHÖNBRUNN

Off stage: Nil

THE FIRST PERFORMANCE OF "THE ABDUCTION FROM THE SERAGLIO"

Off stage: 8 ornate chairs, benches **(Servants)**
Bottle, wine glass **(Venticelli)**

BONNO'S HOUSE

Off stage: Wine glass **(Mozart)**

THE LIBRARY OF THE BARONESS WALDSTÄDTEN

On stage: Large table. *On it:* cakes, desserts **(2 Servants)**
High-backed wing-chair **(2 Servants)**

Off stage: 2 small gilded chairs **(Servants)**
Dressing-robe, shawl **(Servants)**

SALIERI'S APARTMENTS

Off stage: Plate piled with brandied chestnuts **(Cook)**
Portfolio containing manuscripts **(Constanze)**

ACT II

SALIERI'S APARTMENTS

Re-set: Manuscripts in portfolio on chair
Plate of brandied chestnuts on small table

THE PALACE OF SCHÖNBRUNN

Off stage: Nil

VIENNA AND GLIMPSES OF OPERA HOUSES

Off stage: Nil

SALIERI'S APARTMENTS

Off stage: 11 golden upholstered chairs **(Servants)**
Golden satin frock coat. *In pocket:* snuff box **(Valet)**
Gold cake-stand with elaborate cakes **(Cook)**

AN UNLIT THEATRE

Off stage: Figaro score **(Mozart)**

THE THEATRE

Off stage: Nil

THE FIRST PERFORMANCE OF "FIGARO"

Off stage: Nil

THE LIBRARY OF THE BARONESS WALDSTÄDTEN

Off stage: High-backed wing-chair **(Servants)**

VIENNA AND THE PALACE OF SCHÖNBRUNN

Off stage: Nil

THE PRATER

Off stage: Nil

A MASONIC LODGE

Off stage: Masonic apron **(Servant)**

Personal: **Van Swieten:** masonic apron
Mozart: masonic apron

Scene change for MOZART'S APARTMENT; SALIERI'S APARTMENTS

Off stage: Long plain table. *On it:* upturned stool, chair with cushions, blanket,
manuscripts, bottle, quill pen, ink-well, candle **(Servants)**

Personal: **Constanze:** padded apron

THE THEATRE BY THE WEIDEN

Off stage: 2 benches **(Servants)**

Personal: **German crowd:** sausages, pipes
Cavalieri: *mouchoir*

MOZART'S APARTMENT

Off stage: Nil

Scene change for SALIERI'S APARTMENTS

Off stage: Eighteenth-century wheelchair **(Servant)**
Shawl, cap, dressing-robe. *In pocket:* razor **(Servant)**

SALIERI'S APARTMENTS

Off stage: Plate of buns **(Cook)**
2 books, copy of *German Musical Times* **(Venticello 1)**

LIGHTING PLOT

Property fittings required: nil

Various interior and exterior scenes

ACT I

To open: House Lights down

Cue 1	As whispering increases *Gradually bring up lighting upstage to give silhouette effect in the* *Light Box and bring up dim lighting downstage*	(Page 1)
Cue 2	Silk curtains descend *Fade upstage lighting*	(Page 5)
Cue 3	As **Salieri** sings *Bring up House Lights to full*	(Page 5)
Cue 4	**Salieri** kneels *Slowly fade House Lights leaving dim lighting downstage*	(Page 6)
Cue 5	Transformation to the Eighteenth Century *Increase downstage lighting and bring up bright golden effect in* *Light Box*	(Page 7)
Cue 6	When **Emperor** exits *Slightly dim golden effect in Light Box*	(Page 8)
Cue 7	The **Venticelli** exit *Black-out, then quickly bring up downstage lighting and golden* *effect as in previous cue*	(Page 9)
Cue 8	As **Orsini-Rosenberg** leaves the Light Box *Increase downstage lighting slightly*	(Page 10)
Cue 9	**Van Swieten** leaves the Light Box *Fade upstage lighting*	(Page 10)
Cue 10	The Library of the Baroness Waldstädten *Bring up bright interior light in Light Box*	(Page 11)
Cue 11	As **Salieri** runs c *Change to exterior night effect in Light Box and dim downstage* *lighting*	(Page 14)
Cue 12	**Salieri:** ". . . an obscene child!" *Black-out Light Box retaining very dim lighting downstage*	(Page 14)
Cue 13	**Salieri:** ". . . and welcome him myself to Vienna!" *Bring up bright golden light in Light Box and increase downstage* *lighting*	(Page 15)

Cue 14	Alone, **Salieri** moves forward to address the Audience *Fade all lighting to a spot on* **Salieri**	(Page 20)
Cue 15	**Salieri:** "... no danger at all ... Not yet." *Bring up full general lighting*	(Page 20)
Cue 16	**Salieri:** "... had I entertained a notion so sinful!" *Fade on Light Box and dim lighting downstage*	(Page 23)
Cue 17	**Venticello 2:** "At Kappellmeister's Bonno's." *Bring up general lighting in Light Box and increase downstage lighting*	(Page 24)
Cue 18	**Salieri:** "... became more than thought." *Black-out*	(Page 26)
Cue 19	Two simultaneous shouts *Bring up bright effect in Light Box and downstage*	(Page 26)
Cue 20	Light Box curtains descend *Fade lighting in Light Box and retain bright interior effect downstage*	(Page 31)
Cue 21	As soprano sings the "Kyrie" *Gradually bring up clear bright light on* **Salieri**, *growing in intensity*	(Page 35)
Cue 22	After the music has faded *Fade intense bright light—returning to previous downstage lighting*	(Page 35)
Cue 23	As **Salieri** exits *Bring up House Lights*	(Page 36)

ACT II

To open: House Lights and lighting downstage

Cue 24	**Salieri** enters *Fade House Lights*	(Page 37)
Cue 25	**Salieri:** "... my vow of social virtue." *Bring up bright golden light in Light Box*	(Page 39)
Cue 26	**Mozart** moves slowly to the fortepiano *Fade lighting in Light Box and dim downstage lighting*	(Page 40)
Cue 27	**Venticello 2:** "People *faint* with pleasure!" *Bring up lighting in Light Box then fade as* **Salieri** *begins to speak*	(Page 40)
Cue 28	**Venticello 2:** "The cafés are buzzing!" *Bring up lighting in Light Box then fade as* **Salieri** *turns to address the Audience*	(Page 41)
Cue 29	**Venticello 2:** "Throughout all Europe!" *Bring up lighting in Light Box then fade as music stops*	(Page 41)
Cue 30	**Salieri:** "... this house with golden furniture!" *Bring up subdued lighting downstage to give overall gold effect*	(Page 41)

Cue 31	**Salieri** moves away upstage *The Lights begin to dim gradually*	(Page 44)
Cue 32	**Von Strack** joins **Salieri** upstage *The Lights dim further*	(Page 44)
Cue 33	**Joseph:** "Well. *There it is!*" *Bring up overall bright interior lighting*	(Page 48)
Cue 34	**Mozart** rises and walks away *Fade lighting in Light Box and dim downstage lighting*	(Page 50)
Cue 35	**Salieri:** ". . . of his weaknesses." *Bring up bright interior light in Light Box*	(Page 51)
Cue 36	**Salieri:** ". . . the Ghost Father in *Don Giovanni!*" *Fade lighting in Light Box*	(Page 52)
Cue 37	As the two opening chords of *Don Giovanni* sound *Bring up intense light behind Light Box backdrop to give silhouette effect of the Ghost Father*	(Page 52)
Cue 38	**Salieri:** ". . . created only the ordinary." *Fade intense light and silhouette effect*	(Page 52)
Cue 39	**Salieri:** ". . . too hard, surely." *Bring up bright golden light effect in Light Box and increase downstage lighting slightly*	(Page 53)
Cue 40	**Salieri:** (*bowing*) "Majesty." *Dim golden lighting slightly on Joseph*	(Page 53)
Cue 41	**Joseph:** "*Vous nous faîtes honneur!*" *Black-out Light Box*	(Page 53)
Cue 42	**Venticello 2:** "To fill his place." *Bring up golden light in Light Box as before*	(Page 54)
Cue 43	**Joseph:** "—there it is!" *Black-out Light Box*	(Page 55)
Cue 44	**Venticello 2:** "There is, I've seen the mother." *Bring up general lighting and change to give yellow effect*	(Page 55)
Cue 45	**Salieri:** "*Is* he?" *Black-out Light Box and change to general interior effect downstage*	(Page 56)
Cue 46	**Salieri:** "—in a tenement . . ." *Bring up overall general interior lighting*	(Page 62)
Cue 47	**Salieri:** ". . . and burnt away!" *Effect of a great sun rising on the Light Box background with a gigantic silhouette in the middle. Follow with a white fade effect*	(Page 63)
Cue 48	**Van Swieten** and the **Crowd** go out *Black-out Light Box, dim downstage lighting*	(Page 63)
Cue 49	**Salieri** throws open the "door" *Concentrate lighting on Mozart's apartment*	(Page 65)

Cue 50	As the **Citizens of Vienna** enter	(Page 69)
	Increase lighting overall slightly	
Cue 51	**Salieri** sits in the wheelchair	(Page 70)
	Cross fade to give early morning effect downstage	
Cue 52	**Venticello 2:** ".'. . . made away with him by poison.'"	(Page 72)
	Concentrate lighting in a narrow bright cone over **Salieri**	
Cue 53	**The Venticelli** go off	(Page 73)
	Lighting dims slightly	
Cue 54	**Salieri** folds his arms across his breast	(Page 73)
	Fade to Black-out	

PROJECTION PLOT

ACT I

Cue 1   Light box curtains descend   (Page 5)
           Images of long windows on curtains

Cue 2   **Salieri** removes dressing-robe   (Page 7)
           *Fade images on curtains and project golden mirrors fireplace on
           to Light Box backgroud for "Palace"*

Cue 3   **Salieri:** "That night changed my life."   (Page 11)
           *Fade "Palace" projection and replace with image of 2 elegantly-
           curtained windows surrounded by subdued wallpaper for
           "Library"*

Cue 4   **Salieri** runs c   (Page 14)
           *Fade "Library" projection and bring up night street scene on
           Light Box background*

Cue 5   **Salieri:** "... an obscene child!"   (Page 14)
           Fade night street scene

Cue 6   **Salieri:** "... and welcome him myself to Vienna!"   (Page 15)
           Bring up "Palace" projection on Light Box background

Cue 7   Alone, **Salieri** moves forward to address the Audience   (Page 20)
           Fade "Palace" projection

Cue 8   **Salieri:** "... no danger at all ... Not yet."   (Page 20)
           *Bring up line of softly gleaming chandeliers on Light Box
           background for "Theatre"*

Cue 9   **Salieri:** "... had I entertained a notion so sinful!"   (Page 23)
           Fade "Theatre" projection

Cue 10   Two simultaneous shouts   (Page 26)
           Bring up "Library" projection on Light Box background

Cue 11   Light Box curtains descend   (Page 31)
           *Fade "Library" projection and bring up images of long windows
           on curtains*

ACT II

Cue 12   To open Act II   (Page 37)
           Images of long windows on curtains

Cue 13   **Salieri:** "... my vow of social virtue."   (Page 39)
           *Fade images on curtains and bring up "Palace" projection on
           Light Box background*

Cue 14	**Mozart** moves slowly to the fortepiano *Fade "Palace" projection*	(Page 40)
Cue 15	**Venticello 2:** "People *faint* with pleasure!" *Project brilliantly-coloured opera house interior on to Light Box background, then fade as* **Salieri** *begins to speak*	(Page 40)
Cue 16	**Venticello 2:** "The cafés are buzzing!" *Project another opera house interior on to Light Box background, then fade as* **Salieri** *turns to address the Audience*	(Page 41)
Cue 17	**Venticello 2:** "Throughout all Europe!" *Project third opera house interior on to Light Box background then fade as music stops*	(Page 41)
Cue 18	**Von Strack** joins **Salieri** *Project image of lamps glowing faintly in a darkened auditorium on to Light Box background*	(Page 44)
Cue 19	**Joseph:** "Well. *There it is!*" *Fade "Unlit Theatre" and bring up bright theatre auditorium image on Light Box background*	(Page 48)
Cue 20	**Mozart** rises and walks away *Fade "Theatre" image*	(Page 50)
Cue 21	**Salieri:** ". . . of his weaknesses." *Bring up "Library" projection on Light Box background*	(Page 51)
Cue 22	**Salieri:** ". . . the Ghost Father in *Don Giovanni*!" *Fade "Library" projection*	(Page 52)
Cue 23	**Salieri:** ". . . too hard, surely." *Bring up "Palace" image on Light Box background*	(Page 53)
Cue 24	**Joseph:** "*Vous nous faîtes honneur!*" *Black-out "Palace" image*	(Page 53)
Cue 25	**Venticello 1:** "To fill his place." *Bring up "Palace" image*	(Page 54)
Cue 26	**Joseph:** "—there it is!" *Black-out "Palace" image*	(Page 55)
Cue 27	**Venticello 2:** ". . . I've seen the mother." *Bring up image of fresh green trees on Light Box background*	(Page 55)
Cue 28	**Salieri:** "*Is* he?" *Fade tree images*	(Page 56)
Cue 29	**Salieri** sits in the wheelchair *Project images of long windows on to curtains*	(Page 70)
Cue 30	**Salieri** folds his arms across his chest *Fade long window images*	(Page 73)

EFFECTS PLOT

ACT I

Cue 16	**Salieri** looks up at the Audience *Snap off music*	(Page 34)
Cue 17	**Salieri** resumes looking at the manuscript Sinfonia Concertante for Violin and Viola *sounds faintly*	(Page 34)
Cue 18	**Salieri** looks up for the second time *Snap off music*	(Page 34)
Cue 19	**Salieri** resumes reading *Slow movement of the* Concerto for Flute and Harp *sounds*	(Page 35)
Cue 20	**Salieri** looks up for the third time *Snap off music*	(Page 35)
Cue 21	**Salieri:** "... had been no accident." *Faint thundery sound heard in theatre rapidly growing to a thundery roar*	(Page 35)
Cue 22	**Salieri:** "... at an Absolute Beauty!" *See page 35 for effect description*	(Page 35)
Cue 23	The Lights fade and **Salieri** lies quite still *Long pause, then clock strikes eight*	(Page 35)

ACT II

Cue 24	**Salieri:** "At ten o'clock at night!" *Doorbell rings*	(Page 37)
Cue 25	**Mozart** plays and conducts from the fortepiano *Rondo from* Piano Concerto in A Major	(Page 40)
Cue 26	After **Salieri** has bowed for the third time *Snap off music*	(Page 41)
Cue 27	**Salieri:** "... seemed more than coincidence." *End of the third act of* Figaro *sounds faintly*	(Page 47)
Cue 28	**Salieri:** "... been entirely cut." *Snap off music*	(Page 47)
Cue 29	**Salieri:** "And yet I was strangely excited." *Figaro singing faintly "Non piu andrai"*	(Page 49)
Cue 30	**Salieri:** "... to enchant the world forever!" *Fade music, applause*	(Page 49)
Cue 31	**Von Strack:** (*drawling*) "Exactly!" *Bell rings*	(Page 49)
Cue 32	**Salieri:** "... this must remain." *"Ah! Tutti contenti, Saremo Cosi" from* Figaro *heard faintly*	(Page 49)
Cue 33	**Joseph** yawns *Fade music*	(Page 49)
Cue 34	**Salieri:** "... the Ghost Father in *Don Giovanni*!" *First two chords of overture to* Don Giovanni	(Page 52)
Cue 35	**Salieri:** "And I heard *his*—" *"Soave il Vento" from* Cosi Fan Tutte	(Page 52)

Cue 36   **Salieri:** "Hahahahaha!"   (Page 52)
               Snap off music

Cue 37   **Salieri:** "—nothing would!"   (Page 58)
               "Das Klinget so herrlich, Das Klinget so schön!" from The Magic
               Flute *is heard for the scene change*

Cue 38   **Salieri:** "—The Magic Flute."   (Page 62)
               "Heil sei euch Geweihten" from The Magic Flute

Cue 39   **Salieri** points to **Mozart**   (Page 63)
               Fade music

Cue 40   **Salieri:** "... his more terrible clock."   (Page 65)
               Clock strikes one

Cue 41   **Salieri:** "... across the street!"   (Page 65)
               Overture from Don Giovanni

Cue 42   The Lights change instantly   (Page 65)
               Fade music

Cue 43   **Salieri** looks at the manuscript   (Page 66)
               Opening of the Requiem Mass

Cue 44   **Salieri** tears the paper into halves   (Page 66)
               Stop music

Cue 45   **Constanze:** "... wolfi-polfi, please! ..."   (Page 68)
               "Lacrimosa" from the Requiem Mass *begins faintly. Stop where*
               indicated in text

Cue 46   **Constanze** raises her arm in grief   (Page 69)
               Great chord of the "Amen" from the Requiem Mass *sounds and*
               reverberates

Cue 47   **Salieri** sits in the wheelchair and the Lights change   (Page 70)
               Six o'clock strikes

Cue 48   **Salieri:** "Pardon your assassin! Mozart!"   (Page 71)
               Whispers of "Salieri" begin faintly, then increase in volume

Cue 49   **Salieri** cuts his throat   (Page 72)
               Masonic Funeral Music *plays faintly*

Cue 50   **Venticello 2:** '... deluded old man himself.'   (Page 72)
               Stop music

Cue 51   Lights fade to Black-out   (Page 73)
               Last four chords of Masonic Funeral Music

MADE AND PRINTED IN GREAT BRITAIN BY
LATIMER TREND & COMPANY LTD, PLYMOUTH
MADE IN ENGLAND